HOME TO ROOST

HOME TO ROOST

and Other Peckings

DEBORAH DEVONSHIRE

INTRODUCTION BY ALAN BENNETT

Edited by Charlotte Mosley

Drawings by Will Topley

JOHN MURRAY

First published in Great Britain in 2009 by John Murray (Publishers)
An Hachette UK Company

5

Text © Deborah Devonshire 2009
Introduction © Alan Bennett 2009
Illustrations © Will Topley 2009

A CIP catalogue record for this title is available from the British Library

ISBN 978-1-84854-189-4

Typeset in Monotype Bembo by Servis Filmsetting Ltd, Stockport, Cheshire

Printed and bound by Clays Ltd, St Ives plc

John Murray policy is to use papers that are natural, renewable and recyclable
products and made from wood grown in sustainable forests. The logging
and manufacturing processes are expected to conform to the environmental
regulations of the country of origin.

John Murray (Publishers)
338 Euston Road
London NW1 3BH

www.johnmurray.co.uk

To my great-grandchildren
born and as yet unborn

CONTENTS

Introduction by Alan Bennett   I

I Married   7
The Land Agents' Dinner   12
The Small Garden   17
The Organ Recital   21
The Farmers' Club Dinner   23
Derbyshire   30
Lagopus Lagopus Scoticus and its Lodgers   38
Writing a Book   41
Flora Domestica: A History of Flower Arranging,
   1500–1930   45
Book Signings and Literary Lunches   48
The Tulip   51
Unstealables   53
John Fowler: Prince of Decorators   57
Tiaras   61
Auction Catalogues   66
Buying Clothes   70
The Duchess of Devonshire's Ball, 1897   71
A London Restaurant on Trial   74
Edensor Post Office   76
The Arrival of the Kennedys in London, 1938   79
President Kennedy's Inauguration, 1961   83

President Kennedy's Funeral, 1963   93
'The Treasure Houses of Britain' Exhibition in
    Washington   101
Marble Mania   111
Bruce, Mario, Stella and Me   116
Romney Marsh and Other Churches   120
Sassoon: The Worlds of Philip and Sybil   124
Animal Portraits   127
Motorways   129
Memorial Services   133
OFTOF   136
Conservative?   138
Debate at the Cambridge Union   139
Changing Language   141
Deportment   145
Christmas at Chatsworth   146
The Fall and Rise of the Stately Home   151
Cold Houses   154
Recollections of Ditchley and Nancy Lancaster   157
Home to Roost   162

Acknowledgements   167

INTRODUCTION

I knew the minute the call came from Derbyshire that there would be no escape. I had been here before: it was Miss Shepherd all over again.

This might seem unkind, the resemblance between a smelly, deranged and filthily raincoated vagrant and Chatsworth's fragrant chatelaine emeritus not immediately obvious. But they are the same, both strong-willed single-minded women wanting something out of me: Miss Shepherd a haven for her van, the dowager Duchess a foreword for her book. 'Can I bend you to my will?' sister Nancy used to say. Quite.

Note that I have a difficulty calling her Debo (though nobody else does). My acquaintance with duchesses, dowager or otherwise, is scant and feeling it a bit soon after only one meeting to be on first-name terms I settled for Ms Debo while she in her turn called me Mr Alan. I suppose it's a kind of nickname and she is well used to that, the Mitfords having so many nicknames for each other one wonders how they could keep track. Her said sister, Nancy, called her 9, a reference to her supposed mental age; the myth of her own stupidity one that has clung to her all her life and which she still expects us to believe.

Famously unlettered, Ms Debo claims to be like her father who only ever read one book (*White Fang*) and found it so dangerously good he never wanted to read another. And though I feel much the same about opera I don't believe it of Her Grace.

Still it's ironical that having written a story about Someone who discovers the delights of reading I now find I am writing a foreword in praise of Someone Else who never has.

Among the handful of books the author does admit to having read I am delighted to find Priscilla Napier's *A Late Beginner*, a favourite of mine and full of the lost lore and language of nannies. Seeing this recommended, I thought I'd tell her to read Mary Clive's *Day of Reckoning* only to turn the page and find that she already had.

Debo's book ticks so many of my boxes that I'd better start with a mistake (what critics call 'an egregious error') so as not to seem sycophantic. The book begins with a lengthy list of the 11th Duke's offices, appointments and other distinctions ranging from the presidency of Chesterfield and Darley Dale brass bands to being runner-up as White's Club 'Shit of the Year'. However, the list omits (entirely understandably to my mind) the duke's brief sojourn as a governor of Giggleswick School (I think he may have owned the land on which the school is built but that's by the way). This governorship may be a piece of information his relict wishes to suppress as indeed he only attended one governors' meeting, afterwards appearing on the platform in (among other things) yellow socks. Now it happened that the previous day a youth in the sixth form suspected of Bohemian tendencies had been bawled out by his housemaster, the proof of his decadence (and a possible portent of future effeminacy) a pair of yellow socks found in his locker. Following the duke's appearance on the platform, whatever penalties had been imposed were briskly rescinded so there was one boy at least who had cause to bless the name of Cavendish.

Not having read many books has its drawbacks, though it might appal Debo to know that she thereby fulfils one of W. H. Auden's requirements for a budding writer, namely knowing a few books inside out. He would also approve of her fondness for lists and she of his fascination with lead mining and the geology of Derbyshire.

It's a county she revels in. Saddled with her irrepressible Mitford voice she enjoys Derbyshire for its dialect, instancing 'starved' which in Derbyshire means cold. This usage is not confined to Derbyshire, as my mother, who was originally from Halifax, was fond of it. She took it further and applied it to the weather, which she'd describe as 'starvaceous'. 'Mash the tea' is another Derbyshire expression that's shared with Leeds, and it's a handy one too. 'Make the tea' is pretty general and might mean 'Pour it out'. 'Mash the tea' is more precise, meaning 'Put the tea in the pot'. So 'The tea's mashed' means it's just waiting to be poured.

This is a lady who will have seen plenty of teas in her time, teas on terraces, teas in tents, teas with farmers, teas with tenants. She's someone who knows about gooseberries and can discriminate between parsnips. She's on first name terms with her hens, up to the minute on sheep, and pigs, I'm sure, eat out of her hand (which incidentally requires nerve).

To my surprise she's quite charitable about flower arranging, a hobby in my experience that's prone to turn its votaries into hell-hags. 'If you think squash is a competitive activity,' says one of my characters, 'try flower arrangement.'

Though I don't know why I should think it's just flower arrangement: rhubarb growing may be equally cut-throat and I'm sure there's no love lost over leeks and marrows. This is a world Debo has seen much more of than me, having trailed round more than her share of village fêtes and local shows with their ancient categories: 'Three tarts on a plate', 'An edible necklace', or (a favourite, this) 'A garden on a tray', the pond invariably represented by a bit of silver paper.

But there are worlds elsewhere and, surprisingly, one of the most interesting pieces is an essay on tiaras which is not a topic to which I've ever given much thought: I didn't even know that diamonds could be dirty. It's a lovely essay, the kind of vignette you might well have found in the old *New Yorker*.

Debo remembers once having to don the family diamonds, tiara, necklace, stomacher and all, in order to play the lead in the local WI's *The Oldest Miss World in the World* ('My hobbies are hens and world peace'). One just wonders whether she told the insurers.

Both of us having been despatched round provincial book-shops, we share memories of that shaming humiliation of the writer's life, the book-signing.

Writer (pen poised): To whom shall I put it?

Reader (brightly smiling): Me!

Bolder and more pedantic than I've ever dared to be, Debo baulks at signing a book 'To Granny' when it's not her granny, a detail I never let trouble me at all. But I agree with her that anyone who skips a dedication and just wants a signature almost deserves a kiss besides.

Faced with a queue, the staff of the bookshop can get quite bossy ('Her Grace will not be signing bus-tickets'). I'm so anxious to be liked I'm happy to sign bus-tickets and even betting slips if it helps. On one occasion a young man, not having bought the book or anything else, turned round and told me to sign the back of his neck. Which I did. When he next washed I don't like to think.

Deborah Devonshire is not someone to whom one can say, 'Joking apart . . .' Joking never is apart: with her it's of the essence, even at the most serious and indeed saddest moments. At the heart of this collection are three pieces of a different order and all remarkable: diaries of the inauguration of President Kennedy in 1961, of his funeral two years later and an account of the 'Treasure Houses of Britain' exhibition in Washington in 1985.

JFK was a family friend not because famous people know other famous people but through his sister Kathleen (Kick) Kennedy's marriage to Andrew Devonshire's brother, Billy, who was shortly afterwards killed in Belgium. A few years later

Kathleen herself died in a plane crash and is buried at Edensor on the edge of Chatsworth Park. Jack Kennedy was therefore a friend of the family in good times and bad and this brought an invitation to his inauguration as president in January 1961. Reluctant to go (the call of the moors) DD kept a diary of the proceedings, which in their cheerful chaos seem more like India than any English ceremonial.

At one point the newly elected president calls her over to stand beside him while the parade goes by . . . the president having a cup of coffee and a biscuit in gaps between contingents of the three-hour procession. At one point one of the marching troops breaks ranks to take a snap of the president on the podium. The Trooping of the Colour it certainly wasn't.

What's winning is the fun she gets out of it, and a component of the fun she gets out of life is that she seems to have no sense of entitlement. Standing next to the newly inaugurated JFK she thinks of it as an enormous treat and when later he climbs over seven rows of chairs just to have a word, though frozen to the marrow she is in total heaven.

That she is a natural diarist is plain from the oddities that catch her eye, the piece ending as she drifts off to sleep in the British Embassy while outside in the bedroom corridor her husband whispers to the ambassador Sir Harold Caccia the secrets Prime Minister Macmillan had entrusted him to bring over.

Her account of Kennedy's funeral, that terrible Thanksgiving of 1963, is so heartfelt it is difficult to read. Afterwards she is sympathising with the ambassador David Ormsby Gore and his wife. 'It will be very difficult working with the new administration – no intimacy, no shared memories and no jokes.' And the jokes aren't the least of it so that her account of even this wretched weekend manages to end on one. Fog having diverted the funeral party to Manchester, this means a night at Chatsworth where she recalls the (very thin) Prime Minister, Alec Douglas-Home, wondering if perhaps he crept into bed and lay very still she wouldn't have to change the sheets for Princess Margaret who was coming the next day.

I've never thought of Alec Douglas-Home as much of a joker but that's the thing about this lady. She brings it out in people. Good for her.

ALAN BENNETT

I MARRIED

I married:

The twice mayor of Buxton
A Knight of the Garter
The chairman of the Lawn Tennis Association
A parliamentary under-secretary of state
A minister of state in the Commonwealth Relations
    Office
A freeman of the Borough of Eastbourne
A holder of the Military Cross
The chairman of the British Empire Cancer
    Campaign for twenty-five years
The patron-in-chief of the Polite Society
An Old Etonian
A Knight of the Order of St John, Derbyshire
A steward of the Jockey Club
A peer of the realm
A Major in the Coldstream Guards
The patron of twenty-seven livings in the Church
    of England dioceses of Derby, Bradford, Ely,
    Southwell, Chichester, Sheffield and Lincoln
A member of the Horserace Totalisator
    Board
The Vice Lord-Lieutenant of Derbyshire

The prime warden of the Worshipful Company of
   Fishmongers
The author of a book on a famous racehorse
A member of the Garden Society, Society of
   Dilettanti, Grillion's, The Fox Club and The
   Other Club
A graduate of Trinity College, Cambridge
A vice-president of the London Library
The president of the Royal Hospital and Home for
   Incurables, Putney
A soundly beaten Conservative parliamentary
   candidate for Chesterfield in the 1945 and 1950
   general elections
The president of the Devonshire Club, Eastbourne
The president of Derbyshire County Scout Council
The president of the Thoroughbred Breeders'
   Association
A member of the Western European Union,
   Council of Europe
The president of the Royal Commonwealth Society
   (who was sacked after an excellent speech on
   Rhodesia)
The president of the Building Societies Association
A member of the Roxburghe Club
An honorary doctor of law at the University of
   Manchester
A Privy Counsellor
The author of an autobiography
An honorary doctor of law at Memorial University
   of Newfoundland
The president of the Matlock and Eastbourne
   branches of Mencap
A vice-president of the All England Lawn Tennis
   and Croquet Club

A member of Brooks's, White's, the Beefsteak and
the Turf Club

An honorary doctor of law at the University of
Salford

The president of the National Deaf Children's
Society

The first peer to join the Social Democratic Party,
which he left to sit on the crossbenches in the
House of Lords (and was then abolished)

The Master of the Worshipful Company of Farriers

The runner-up in White's Club 'Shit of the Year',
Private Eye, 1974

The president of the Royal National Institute for
the Blind

The chancellor of the University of Manchester

The major shareholder in Heywood Hill Bookshop
and founder-donor of the Heywood Hill Literary
Prize

A president of the Bakewell Agricultural and
Horticultural Society

The president of the Conservative Friends of Israel

The president of Derbyshire County Cricket Club

An honorary doctor of law at the University of
Liverpool

A front bench spokesman in the House of Lords on
transport

The president of the National Council for One
Parent Families

The patron of the Barnardo's Year of the Volunteer,
1986

The president of the Longshaw Sheepdog Trials

The president of the Federation of West Derbyshire
Mental Health Support Groups

The proprietor and chairman of Pratt's Club

An honorary Colonel of Manchester and Salford
    Universities' Officer Training Corps
The president of the African Medical and Research
    Foundation (which runs the Flying Doctor
    Service)
An honorary member of the French Jockey Club
The president of Chesterfield Football Club
The president of Eastbourne College
A trustee of the National Gallery
The chairman of the Chatsworth Estates Company
The president of Chesterfield and Darley Dale Brass
    Bands
A man after whom a variety of sweet pea was
    named
The patron of the Midland Cairn Terrier Club

I have changed my name three times but I have only been married once.

Deborah Mitford (1920–) married, in 1941, Lord Andrew Cavendish (1920–2004). In 1944, on the death of his elder brother, Andrew inherited the courtesy title of Marquess of Hartington. After his father's death in 1950, he became the 11th Duke of Devonshire. In spite of being a government spokesman on transport, he never held a driving licence; he was never the owner of a Cairn terrier and was piqued at being voted only runner-up for the White's Club award (Lord Lambton was the winner). This list of his offices and distinctions is by no means exhaustive.

THE LAND AGENTS' DINNER

Anyone who chooses land agency as a profession has to know everything about everything, from drains to fine arts, from roads to Rembrandts. He must be able to talk in their own terms to lawyers and loonies, gamekeepers and golfers, ploughmen and planners, prime ministers and policemen. Land agents can do just that and a thousand other things besides; they are the people who cheerfully face the problems that will affect the future spirit and appearance of the country and the villages to which we are all devoted.

They and their wives have to be ready to face any emergency. The great-aunt of a friend of mine was married to the Sandringham agent during the reign of King Edward VII. Queen Alexandra used to wander into the houses round about, taking with her whatever guests she had staying. One day, the agent's wife was, as usual, bent double in her garden when the maid came rushing out shouting, 'Come quickly. Come quickly. There are THREE QUEENS in the hall and I don't know what to do with them.'

At Chatsworth we have been very lucky in the marvellous people who have ruled in the estate office. Until my father-in-law died, there were seven agents spread around the country from Carlisle to Eastbourne. His mother, Evelyn Duchess of Devonshire, carried on a running fight with all of them. She loved interfering almost as much as I do. The unlucky Hugo

Read, who looked after Hardwick Hall where she lived, was the recipient of many a sharp note, usually on her favourite subjects of woodworm, dry rot and drains. She stayed on at Hardwick after 1957 when the government took it for death duties and transferred it to the National Trust. In her eighties, she became a prime exhibit herself, always joining the visitors for tea. On the subject of the tearoom, Hugo received the following note from her: 'Mrs Norton still makes her horrid little pink tarts, but they seem to have been enjoyed by two Nottingham businessmen.'

Her husband, Victor, the 9th Duke of Devonshire, was a real countryman. He loved cricket and when he saw to his distress that, in spite of a large intake of likely lads in the way of sub-agents and pupils, the Chatsworth cricket team was not doing too well, he got annoyed with Mr Hartopp, the agent. In desperation, the latter put an advert in several local papers which read: 'Wanted. Plumber for estate maintenance work. Must be a good wicket-keeper.'

The duke's head agent, Sir Roland Burke, was also honorary director of the Royal Show and for many years it was more or less run from the Chatsworth estate office. Burke served his apprenticeship at the Royal, starting in the lowly role of assistant steward in the Poultry Tent and ending up kneeling on the straw in the showground to be knighted by the King. When my father-in-law succeeded, one of the first things he decided to do was to get rid of Roland Burke. He couldn't bear him. But the difficulty was how to do it. My father-in-law was a very kind man and rather shy. He spent ages composing a speech for the awful interview. He decided to hang it on economy and made up a long rigmarole about how the estate could no longer afford the luxury of a head agent. Burke arrived and the duke began, 'Regretfully it is necessary to make some cuts and economies . . .' but before he could get any further, Roland interrupted and said, 'I have been thinking along the same lines and realise that

13

economies have to be made. Therefore, I am quite prepared to sacrifice my third groom.'

Those of us who live and work in the country must all be acquainted with autocratic and authoritative gamekeepers – a race apart, who are accustomed to special privileges because of their special position. At Chatsworth there reigned for forty-five years the ultimate in the profession – one John Maclauchlan. He lived in a house with a Paxtonian tower, had his own chauffeur and called the Duke of Portland 'His Other Grace'. He and the old Duke of Devonshire used to tool round the country in the back of a huge brown Rolls-Royce (not that the duke ever referred to it as such but would order the 'Stink Hog' to be brought round). It was driven by Mr Burdekin, the duke's chauffeur, whose instructions were never to exceed 25 miles per hour. On the rare occasions when he went a little faster, Victor would bang on the glass partition with his stick and shout, 'Burdekin, Burdekin, what do you think you are, a crazy cow with a tin tied on its tail?'

Maclauchlan had the ear of the duke and always got his own way. He heartily despised Sir Roland Burke and the other agents. Once when King George V was shooting at Chatsworth, the King turned round before the start of the best drive to see a group of eight or nine men standing, as he thought, uncomfortably close. 'Who are those men?' he asked Maclauchlan. 'Oh, take no notice of them, Your Majesty. They are just a posse of agents. Shoot them if you like.' When Andrew and I first went to live in the village of Edensor, next to Chatsworth, Mr Maclauchlan sent for me (there was no suggestion of his coming to our house). I arrived, of course, at the right time, was shown into the parlour by his daughter and the great man entered. 'Lady Hartington,' he said, 'I have sent for you to tell you that you can go wherever you like.'

I often think Victor Duke and my father would have made wonderful keepers. Victor would have been a tremendously conscientious and steady beat keeper, and my father would have been a terrifying head keeper with his entrenching tool at the ready. Poachers would have been what the newspapers describe as 'at risk' in his domain. Both men understood the ways of birds and beasts but neither was what my father called 'literary coves'. My father would not have wasted time reading – a trait I have inherited from him and one which made my sister Nancy call me '9', as she said that was my mental age. She used to address envelopes to me as '9 Duchess of Devonshire' and introduced me to her smart French friends as 'my 9-year-old sister' when I was well over forty.

My father's attitude to reading was most sensible. He only ever read one book and that was *White Fang*. He loved it so much he never read another because nothing could ever be as good. 'Dangerous good book,' he used to say, 'no point in trying any more.' I remember an unfortunate woman coming to lunch with my parents. The reason I remember is because no one outside the family was ever asked, so it was a very special occasion. The poor soul was ugly, something my father didn't allow – the sort of woman he called 'a meaningless piece of meat'. It was the time when everyone was talking about Elinor Glyn and her work. Casting round for a subject to break the silence, I heard our guest say, 'Lord Redesdale, have you read *Three Weeks*?' My father glared at her. 'I haven't read a book for *three years*,' he replied (an exaggeration as it had been twenty since he had read *White Fang*).

How surprised my grandfather-in-law and my father would be at the change in standards of housing in the country now. They didn't live to see bathrooms, let alone the double garage, central heating and downstairs lavatory which are now the order of the day. The two men were like a very ancient friend of mine who invited me to shoot in Gloucestershire recently. We were walking through a wood, miles from anywhere, when we came upon a ruined cottage – just a chimney stack, a couple of steps and a heap of stones. My friend looked lovingly at it and said, 'It's the most extraordinary thing, you know, you can't get a feller to live in a place like that any more.'

They would have understood Mr Hey, our beloved friend who looked after Bolton Abbey for many years and who in old age grew to look exactly like the grouse he loved. Mr Hey was, to say the least, careful with money. He was once telling me about a tenant who was getting restive about the length of time it was taking to put a bathroom into his house. 'We really must do something for him,' I said. 'Well, I've given him a shower.' '*Have* you, Mr Hey?' 'Yes, I've taken a slate off the roof.' He used to send the most fearsome bills after our annual stay at Bolton Abbey, every conceivable item written into them, almost including the air we breathed. The last line was always the same: 'Mousetraps – 9d.' I could never understand why we couldn't reuse the ones from last year. But that's agents for you, they have to balance their books somehow.

January 1983

THE SMALL GARDEN
by C. E. Lucas Phillips

Of the vast number of books on gardening – fat, shiny and heavy with photographs – that fill our shelves this has long been my favourite. First published in 1952, it met a post-war enthusiasm for beautifying your plot. This reprint is good news indeed.

The author was a handsome Brigadier, decorated for distinguished service in both world wars. He was also an inspired writer, an original who holds the attention of the reader with his instructions on even the duller aspects of gardening. He tells us he is an amateur writing for amateurs. Too modest, but it is an encouragement to beginners and succeeds in making us want to try to get it right.

It is nothing if not thorough. The basics are explained, the step-by-step stages that lead to the pleasure of growing whatever you fancy, for anyone who knows one end of a hoe from the other. There is a glossary and a cultural calendar (it is a comfort to see 'cultural' used in this context and not coupled with 'heritage', describing some outrageous kind of art). Lucas Phillips tackles the vexed problem of plant names in the same robust way as the other difficulties met in learning how to deal with the vegetable kingdom. Many of his instructions are positively poetic: compost, its components and how to mix them, the value of liquid manure of a 'deep tawny hue' (but when it comes to adding 'a trifle of soot' you may have to admit defeat should your house be without coal fires). Other unlikely subjects are so well described they carry you along with intense pleasure.

There is much to go into before you dig. Fifty pages go by before he puts spade, fork and hoe to the earth. There are some surprises in the chapter on tools ('The Gardener's Armoury'): 'the dibber should be handled with care . . . in unskilled hands it is a menace to the infant plant.' I never looked on the good old dibber as a menace but his reason for the warning is logical.

The seasons and the work they bring are explained in simple language you cannot forget. Digging and manuring in the autumn allows the frosts to break up newly dug clods, working on particles of soil moisture as it does on water pipes, bursting and crumbling heavy soil into a fine tilth with great efficiency. The comparison to domestic burst pipes brings this process of nature home to every British householder. Early-spring east winds, with their 'harrowing breath', bring you to the coming of summer and the author begs you not to disturb the roots of established plants when keeping the ground clear of invaders, but a little light hoeing 'to slaughter the weeds' is in order.

I know of no other gardening book that engages our interest in subjects dull as ditch water and vaguely unpleasant as well, apt to be skipped in search of something more attractive. You have to read on for fear of missing some descriptive gem and you remember what he says because of how he says it. His language gets better and better. Cuckoo-spit: 'inside a mass of frothy spittle is a curious soft creature which on disturbance will attempt to escape by weak hops.' You can't beat it.

He is at his most lyrical describing the plants he loves. The lesser known species anemones, for instance, 'have a chaste and porcelain beauty', fragile and virginal. *Eremurus* are 'elegant ladies of hyacinthine appearance of 6 ft stature and more. Expensive . . . Beware slugs.' The best he can say of the easily grown Valerian is 'Beloved by Winston Churchill'. He does not spare us his dislikes and warns that after flowering in 'barbaric splendour' in late spring, the Oriental poppy is a 'grizzly mess'. You can't have one without the other. *Salvia splendens* is a 'pillar-box red bedding plant which startles the optic nerve in August'. Cecil Beaton had the same anti-scarlet prejudice and called this salvia and its colour-mates 'retina irritants'.

The pages on roses produce their own loving descriptions. How Lucas Phillips would have enjoyed the modern tribe of new/old roses which answer all needs with their scent, vigour and complicated beauty. Looking to a brighter future, he barks out orders to amputate newly planted ramblers to within 15 inches of the ground, thus preventing any flowers in their first year, and makes sure we obey by adding that this is 'a cardinal injunction not to be funked'.

Much of the Brigadier's writing is delightfully dated. Many bright little plants are 'gay' and in my battered old paperback he recommends a dependable insecticide, DDT – edited out of this edition now it is illegal. Slugs, bugs and bacteria are likened to Fifth Columnists. The new generations of gardeners may wonder at the meaning of that. Weeds are classed in three degrees of abomination, the worst being the tap-rooted varieties, 'underground creeping horrors'. Couch grass and ground elder are 'vegetative serpents, brutes which laugh at the hoe as love laughs at the locksmith'.

The chapter on the kitchen garden takes us steadily along, with all the favourites and their needs clearly described. It is embellished with simple line-drawings (we have already seen a little masterpiece entitled 'How Not to Water'); one page ends with 'a gallery of oddments', which show their age as today they are no longer odd but fashionable – kohlrabi, celeriac and salsify.

Having profited by the Lucas Phillips wisdom and followed his ways in making a new garden – or improving an old one – to our (and his) liking, we arrive at the last chapters, where he excels himself. 'Know Your Enemy', something the old soldier studied in his military career and applies forcibly to the deceptive calm of the garden, is his title for the introduction to this section. Who could forget the picture conjured up by scab and canker 'going hand in hand'? It cries out for a drawing by Edward Lear of these brotherly pests advancing on your apple trees. He quotes Erasmus Darwin in 1790, 'Crack follows crack, to laws elastic just / And the frail fabric shivers into dust.'

We are jolted into full attention by the originality and often hilarious descriptions of 'Friend and Foe' and, best of all, 'The Enemy in Detail'. Who else but our now beloved author would describe the larva of the ladybird (a friend) as 'agile, torpedo-shaped, resembling a minute crocodile'? You have got to learn the difference between the 'brisk' centipede (friend) and a millipede (foe). The latter has 'innumerable very small legs and, when worried, gives off an obnoxious smell from his stink glands'. The idea of a 'worried' millipede is something I have never considered but I will now – assuming I can tell it apart from its fewer legged rival, the friendly centipede – and I will do my best to give the former a nervous breakdown. I am afraid the children's dear old tortoise is entirely an enemy.

The worst garden pest by a long way is Man ('ignorant and lazy'), led in his assault on nature by the Jobbing Gardener. (Fifty years on, would the worst pest be the strimmer?) Birds are in a special category and have become 'a serious problem . . . pestiferous to fruit'. RSPB please note.

Dip into this book and you will find yourself digging. Dig and you will be rewarded.

2006

THE ORGAN RECITAL

When two or three old people are gathered together in the name of lunch, you can be sure of the subject of conversation to start the ball rolling. Illnesses of all shapes and sizes are the thing and the Organ Recital* begins. Heads, bodies and legs are dissected; noses, throats and ears, skin and bones, arteries, liver and lights, and (Blair's favourites) hearts and minds. Once you start on minds you are in for a basinful. Of the two it is better to stick to hearts and whether or not you are allowed to walk upstairs.

Hips and knees lead to bones. Stomachs, teeth and gums, closely allied as it is not much use having one without the others, can lead to a dissertation on dentistry. Impacted wisdom teeth are good but there is a trick called root canal treatment that takes almost as long to describe as the lengthy treatment itself, with your jaws jammed open till the cows come home. There is a strong sense of competition, even as to the waiting time at hospital (length of); tales of woe are capped and re-capped as the Organ Recital progresses.

Various syndromes that I've never heard of are trotted out as a part of everyday life and sympathy is expected from the listener. Doctors come in for praise or criticism. Surgeons are either haloed magicians or bunglers who ought to be struck off. A curious thing is that they are always described as 'my GP' or 'my surgeon', when they are ordinary independent people who don't belong to anyone. Consultants are described as 'you know who

21

I mean, the big kidney man' or whatever the man's favourite bit of body happens to be.

Look out when it comes to food, which is either very good or very bad for you. Lumped together as 'diet' it is dangerous ground because the dish you are giving someone for lunch will have come in for a pounding before they sit down to it. An extraordinary phenomenon, unknown to our parents, is fads. An invitation, especially to a municipal or university celebration, often has 'Special Dietary Requirements' printed on it, with a space for you to fill in. What you and I never see are the replies, so we don't ever know if the invitees just put 'caviar'.

If a grand person is among the guests, his/her PA will telephone to say, 'I thought you would like to know that X cannot eat . . .' and then follow all the most delicious foods one after another. Next time this happens I plan to say, 'Why can't they just say "no thank you"?' If the guest is very grand indeed and suffers from some strange religion, there is little you can safely offer. Better steer clear as such social life has become full of pitfalls.

You must leave at least ten minutes for the Organ Recital, which leads seamlessly, as they say now (what are these non-existent seams that people go on about?), to Trolley Talk, the romance of the aisles, the thrill of the checkout, the way favour-ites are repackaged or moved round the supermarket and hidden from the most determined shopper. You will be lucky if you get away with six minutes on this subject. Then you can agree how wonderful it is that we never hear of Blair now and what a pity it was that Mr Cameron ever mentioned grammar schools.

August 2008

---

* An expression borrowed from the late Lord Annan.

THE FARMERS' CLUB DINNER

Thank you very much for asking me to come here tonight. I do not know how I dared accept but I was blinded by flattery and, as usual in these cases, the invitation came some time ago so I was sure I would be dead by now. The people at this dinner are the cleverest in the world in the profession I admire most in the world, and I ought to have known that if by some strange chance I was still alive, the terror of my role would induce a heart attack. But to propose the toast to Agriculture and the Farmers' Club is a tremendous honour and one I appreciate more than I can say.

The only people who ever ask me to give a talk are the Women's Institutes, usually the ones very near at hand and always in January and February when they think a proper speaker might get stuck in the snow. A few years ago I wouldn't have been bold enough to do even that but I was thrown in at the deep end. I was staying with a friend in Sussex who is secretary of her local WI. The day of the meeting coincided with my visit and a secretary's nightmare happened: the speaker failed. Faced with an expectant audience and nothing doing, she said, 'YOU must talk.' 'I *can't*,' I protested, 'what on earth could I talk about?' 'Tell them about Chatsworth,' she said. 'I *can't* . . .' In the end I did. They were bored to death. In deep Sussex I'm sure they'd never heard of Derbyshire, let alone Chatsworth. But polite as the WI always are, they listened to the end of this awful experience. When we got home I asked my friend what the real talk should have been about. She got the programme down from the mantelpiece and the title was, 'Ramblings of an Old Woman'. So that is what you're getting tonight.

The reason I feel so proud to be here is because the people who work the land are the men I like and admire more than any others – especially the men of the hills and hard weather, men who live for and by their land, their cattle and their sheep, who are not ruled by clocks and train times, who are not parasites living off other people's efforts, or critics (except of course of governments), who are not always looking over their shoulder wondering what other people are thinking of them, but are totally independent and go about their hard and exacting tasks according to the seasons, as their fathers and forefathers did before them. They are the men who do the work and they are the men who command my respect.

Since marrying and moving to Derbyshire during the war, I have been surrounded by such people. Several characters stand out: one was George Hambleton, who died not long ago at a ripe old age. He had walked a Shire stallion and then became a cowman. Little is said or written about the stockmen, horsemen and shepherds whose lives are spent with the animals in their charge. On them depends the welfare of the stock, and therefore the success or failure of their division of the farm. George was one of those men who understood his animals by instinct and was in total sympathy with them. He could see at once if there was anything wrong and was as good as any vet at diagnosis – and as good as any nurse at treating the ailment. Hours mean nothing to such men – cows don't calve to order during weekdays and it would never occur to them to be absent at crucial times. George was quietly critical of some of the young men, fresh from agricultural college, who thought they knew the lot. 'They don't know as much as they think they do,' he once said to me, 'well, *some don't even know what a swingle tree is.*' Such are the people who produce the superb stock for which this country is renowned.

No praise or thanks can be high enough for them and no men expect it less.

Anyone born after George's generation will be puzzled by all the horse expressions in our language – kicking over the traces, working against the collar, taking the bit between the teeth, being trotted out, keeping on a tight rein, put out to grass, can't take his oats – all from a lost world where the horse and its ways were an essential part of life. Gone too are the binders, stooks and ricks, and the threshing days when all the boys in the village enjoyed going ratting. With the changing look of farming, the poets must also change when writing about the country. The first line of Kipling's 'L'Envoi':

There's a whisper down the field where the year has shot her yield
And the ricks stand grey to the sun.

would have to read:

There's a whisper down the field where the year has shot her yield
And the plastic bags shine black to the sun.

Not quite the same thing somehow.

My husband's grandfather, the 9th Duke of Devonshire, loved his farm and his Shires and Shorthorns far more than the extraordinary works of art he lived among. He was no beauty, and was what could be described as 'of bucolic appearance'. The Royal Show, which at that time moved to a different place annually, was one of the highlights of his year. When it was held at Newcastle, the sleeper train from London waited in a siding till it was a reasonable time for its passengers to get up (railways sought to please their customers in those days). Two farmers walking down the platform saw the recumbent figure of the duke, sound asleep in true Cavendish fashion, his pink head on a pillow. 'That's a fine Large White,' said one farmer. 'That's no Large White, that's the Duke of Devonshire,' answered his companion – a Derbyshire man, no doubt, who could tell the difference.

The duke kept diaries which are a joy to read and are an antidote to the wordy ways of our masters, the bureaucrats of today. Many entries referred to Shire horses and cows. One describes an equine tragedy in just six words: 'Tremendous thunderstorm. Mother Hubbard dropped dead.' Others read: 'Butterfly cast her calf. Very troublesome.' 'Mrs Drewry's funeral – sad little ceremony. Much warmer. Shot a few rooks after.' 'Went to see the new church at Flookborough. Thought it rather askew.' But my favourite entry, headed 'London', reads: 'Important meeting in Buxton. Missed train. Rather glad.'

Nowadays, the third Saturday in September is one of the most important days in the year for Chatsworth Farms. It is the day of the sheep sale and, in four hours or so, the harvest of that enterprise is gathered in. I am told it is the biggest one-day sale from a single owner in the country. At daybreak the shepherds start to pen some 6,000 sheep in a field above Edensor. Cattle lorries squeeze up the lane where the notice 'Unfit for Cars' is covered by a fertiliser bag. Children play in tiers of straw-bale seats before the tent begins to fill with men whose Breughel-like faces proclaim their intimacy with the long English winters.

Ian Lawton, the auctioneer, stands in his stall and gives an inimitable performance, like the conductor of an orchestra with a bit of Mr Punch thrown in, stabbing and embracing the air while reciting his exhortations to the expressionless company at breakneck speed. 'Look sharp or they'll walk away. Listen to me now. Keep waving, sir. £37.80 settles it. Square 'em up. There's a lot of service in these. Away they go. A change of tup now and we have Bleu de Maine . . .' At the same time he is able to spot the bidders, invisible to you and me, most of whom have announced they will not be buying today, the lambs are far too dear. Ian keeps up his virtuoso one-man show for three and a half hours without a break, and his gavel, bound in layers of sticking plaster, bangs down ninety times an hour, as the same number of pens, each holding twenty to twenty-five sheep, is funnelled through the sawdust ring. I would give a lot to see him on the rostrum at Christie's. He would make the Bond Street dealers sit up and look sharp or the Rembrandts would walk away: 'Here come the Botticellis, sound in reed and udder, change the tup and you'll get a Van Gogh . . .'

Chatsworth has a Farm Shop, which, although successful, does produce some rather odd complaints. I have had two letters from women who bought a whole lamb for their freezers. Their messages were the same: 'When I drive through the park at Chatsworth, I see the lambs and they have four legs. When I unpacked the lamb I bought from you it had only two legs. What happened to the other two?' Farmers looking for diversification please note – breed a sheep with four legs, forget the shoulders and you'll be made!

This rambling old woman has seen strange changes in the world of agriculture. It seems only yesterday when farmers were heroes, the growers and providers of our food during and after the war. Now we seem to have turned into the enemy, the spoilers of landscapes (which, by the way, farmers invented), poisoners, torturers, perpetrators of all that is wicked. If that wasn't enough, a new language has been foisted on us, impossible for a simpleton like me to understand or keep up with because it is always being added to. Gatts and Caps, Variables and Clawbacks, now Iaccs – all too difficult. The hours of work and frustration caused by hordes of pressure groups, led by well-meaning, single-issue, muddle-headed people who are not countrymen and find it hard to understand the processes of nature, are unbelievable. I'm sure you all know the kind I mean and suffer from them.

Arising out of the enthusiasm of these new rural dwellers, I confidently expect the ones we know will soon be joined by Save the Rat Society, the Protection of Maiden Aunts in the Country Association, Family Planning for Rabbits (this will need a large staff), the Barbed Wire Heritage Group, the Single-Parent Frog Club, the Married Deer Association of Great Britain, the Society for the Rights of Moles and the World Fund for the Promotion of Dry Rot (the Wet Rot Club will be the junior branch). I look forward to hearing from the secretaries of these fruiting bodies, all of whom will be asking for £1 million to get going. I am longing for the findings of a government enquiry into the Fouling of Fields by Farm Stock, and the ensuing legislation which may be difficult to enforce, and new regulations making it illegal for anyone to go out of doors without wearing rubber gloves. But the best of the new societies is a London one. I'm proud to say my sister-in-law is its president. It is called the Society for Neutering Islington's Pussies – SNIP for short.

My family and I spend August at Bolton Abbey, in a magical spot in Yorkshire, where the straight-talking people are economical with words but not with the truth. A man who lives at the end of our lane is wonderfully gloomy. Once, when we had just arrived, he was telling me of the changes in the village during the year. 'So, how's the new postman getting on?' I asked. 'The new postman?' Pause. 'He's made a bad start.' Long pause. 'He's dead.'

I think you'll all be dead if I don't stop, so may I thank you again for a lovely dinner in excellent company and ask you to rise for the toast: 'Agriculture and the Farmers' Club.'

December 1991

DERBYSHIRE

I was brought up on the borders of Oxfordshire and Gloucestershire and have the unassailable affection for that beautiful part of England that everyone who has had a happy childhood feels for their native heath. When I moved to Derbyshire in 1943, Andrew was with his regiment in Italy and I settled into our first proper home in Ashford-in-the-Water with a baby, a pony and cart, two dogs and a pig.

I thought I should never get used to the scale of the Derbyshire landscape, to the size of the hills and valleys, to the hardness of the stone walls, bare of stonecrop and lichen, and to the length of the winters in a climate where May can be as cold as February. I have lived in the county now for nearly forty years and have grown to love the space and the remote places and would not change them for any other.

There is infinite variety in Derbyshire. Some of the most important quarries and related heavy industry in England are just a few miles from high, lonely, limestone hills, criss-crossed by light grey, drystone walls. Thorn and ash trees, bent to the wind, grow along the wall sides, and limestone outcrops show through the thin soil in the sudden rocky clefts of the dales. It is a landscape like no other in England, where you can find globe-flower, Jacob's ladder, water avens, several kinds of orchid and even lily-of-the-valley growing wild. There are old lead mines, windswept villages of stout stone buildings, and incomparable views of a green and grey landscape inhabited by sheep and ubiquitous Friesian cows. The scenery of the dales is made more dramatic near Buxton and Wirksworth by immense quarries, the man-made cliffs outdoing the natural ones, and just as beautiful in their own way – Derbyshire's answer to the white cliffs of Dover.

Another kind of lonely countryside is the moorland around the Derwent Dams, those engineering marvels of man-made lakes surrounded by heathery hills and indigenous woodland. The stone buildings of the dams have a monumental quality and look as permanent as the hills themselves. This is the home ground of the Woodland Whiteface sheep, an ancient breed that was nearly extinct a few years ago until revived interest in rare breeds ensured its survival.

The start of the Pennine Way is at Edale and so popular has this walk become that the paths have grown wider and wider, and the heather and other vegetation is receding under the thousands of feet that pound it every year. Ill-prepared hikers can get a fright when the weather changes without warning, soaking them in rain and enveloping them in mist, with visibility down to the end of your nose. The Way crosses the well-named Bleaklow and Black Ashop Moor, as well as Kinder Scout, 2,088 feet above sea level, where the Mass Trespass of 1932 created famous (and often quoted) publicity for the ramblers, when six of their number were arrested for 'riotous assembly'. Kinder Scout is the highest point of this inhospitable but fascinating country of grouse moors and hill sheep, where shepherds and their collies rule, and where the high road of the Snake Pass is the first to be closed by snow every winter.

If the hills are remarkable, so are the rivers. In 1817, Lord Byron wrote to the Irish poet Thomas Moore, 'Was you ever in Dovedale? I can assure you there are things in Derbyshire as noble as Greece or Switzerland.' Izaak Walton and Charles Cotton spent most of their lives in happy contemplation of the Dove, 'the finest river that I ever saw, and the fullest of fish', wrote Walton. Another crystal-clear trout stream is the Wye, which rises near Buxton and runs through Miller's Dale, Ashford-in-the-Water and Bakewell, underneath Haddon Hall to join the Derwent at Rowsley. The most exciting stretch of the Wye is Monsal Dale, where the tall railway viaduct links the hills. The viaduct is a prime example of the changes in fashion in what is admired and what is denigrated. John Ruskin was infuriated when it was built in 1863 and by what he considered the ruination of the dale, just so that 'every fool in Buxton can be in Bakewell in half an hour and every fool at Bakewell in Buxton'. Now it is revered as a triumph of engineering and for its own regular beauty.

The very names of the villages invite a closer look: Parsley Hay, Chapel-en-le-Frith, Alsop-en-le-Dale, Dove Holes, Peak Forest, Monyash, Foolow, Edensor, Stoney Middleton, Hope, Fenny Bentley, Stanton-in-Peak, Thorpe Cloud, Wigley, Earl Sterndale; and the dales: Chee Dale, Miller's Dale, Deep Dale, Monk's Dale, Demon's Dale, Cressbrook Dale, Lathkill Dale, Crackendale, Beresford Dale and many more.

There are caves, notably Poole's Hole near Buxton and the Great Rutland Cavern under the Heights of Abraham at Matlock Bath, a restored seventeenth-century lead mine in working order. The wealth produced from lead mining was of great importance to the county and the Barmote Courts, where lead-mining disputes were settled, are still held at Wirksworth and other places. Carved tablets showing miners' tools adorn the front of Wirksworth Moot Hall and the big brass dish used as a measure for lead ore since 1513 is preserved here.

The mineral unique to Derbyshire is Blue John, the yellow and blue fluorspar which for centuries has been made into urns, ornaments and even tabletops, as well as smaller objects such as knife handles and jewellery. It is thought to have got its name from the French *bleu jaune*. Blue John pieces are high fashion in antique shops and the prices are as steep as the descent into the

Blue John mines, which you enter under the shadow of Peveril Castle at Castleton. The Peak Cavern (or Devil's Arse) has the largest cave entrance in Britain. In the Speedwell Cavern you travel for half a mile in a boat on the underground canal, and Treak Cliff Cavern is remarkable for its stalactites and stalagmites. Small quantities of Blue John are still extracted.

There is silence and solitude in the uplands of the Peak District, where once the Blue John and lead mines were worked by families as true cottage industries, in contrast with the coal mines around Chesterfield and Clay Cross, and the iron and heavy industries of Staveley, Alfreton and adjacent towns, where the night was lit by flames from the chimneys of the works that carried on their noisy trade twenty-four hours a day. Good arable land runs alongside opencast coal works, reminding us that industry and farming have coexisted in the county since the Romans worked the lead mines.

In 1771, Sir Richard Arkwright set up the first successful water-powered cotton mill in Cromford. Today there is great interest in industrial archaeology and the Arkwright Society has preserved some of the mills for visitors to see. One of the most hauntingly beautiful mills is on the River Wye at Cressbrook, which you come upon unexpectedly in a secluded narrow dale. Another impressive one is at Calver on the Derwent. It was used as Colditz Castle in the 1970s BBC television series and was a realistic model for that grim edifice. The National Tramway Museum at Crich is fascinating, full of memories for grown-ups and of wonder for children.

Derbyshire is physically and psychologically divided into north and south round about Matlock, where the Midlands seem to end and the north begins. This was recognised soon after the war, when local government offices were moved from Derby to the old spa hotel buildings in Matlock, a much more convenient centre from which to administer the long, narrow county. At Matlock accents change and the scenery turns from productive corn land into harsher, higher, grass country. You climb to a height of 1,000 feet before you reach Buxton in the north, where the 5th Duke of Devonshire and Carr of York built the glorious Crescent. Here the average mean temperature in July is 57.5° F – mean indeed! No wonder the inhabitants delighted in the warm mineral springs. Buxton and Matlock were important spas when such treatment was fashionable.

Alas, the baths are no more. I have an abiding memory of a happy afternoon in a peat bath at Buxton, a 'perk' of the mayoress, which I was at the time. It was the colour and consistency of a huge cowpat. I lay in it up to my neck, sweating happily, till ordered out by the attendant who then sprayed me with a jet of clean, cold water to remove the beneficial but clinging brown stuff. I never felt better or smoother-skinned in my life and I rue the passing of the baths.

The denizens of Derbyshire are not as restless as those in the south. Some years ago our local doctor did a survey of the village of Hartington to try to discover more about goitre, or Derbyshire Neck as it is called from the commonness of the disease in this neighbourhood. He found that 90 per cent of the people living in the village were born there, a statistic unlikely to be equalled farther south. Surnames like Wildgoose and Burdekin, which are not uncommon round here, never fail to surprise 'foreigners'. In Derbyshire you don't make tea, you 'mash' it. If someone says he's 'starved', he means he's cold, not hungry. I know several natives who say 'thee' instead of 'you'. My daughter at a Pony Club camp on the outskirts of a remote Peakland village once heard the farmer threaten his erring son, 'Eh John, if thee don't shape theeself I'll belt thee one.' Some swear words have never had the meaning given to them farther south – at any rate, they sound different in a Derbyshire voice. When Andrew stood for Parliament, a friend came to Chesterfield from London to canvass. She asked the driver who met her at the station how Andrew was getting on. 'They like 'im but they say booger 'is party', was the answer. Andrew's candidature was never successful but there is no better way of getting to know a town and its inhabitants than to be a candidate. I have a deep affection for the place and still have many friends there.

The dilapidated Victorian Market Hall in Chesterfield and the shops on Low Pavement nearly succumbed to being put in a giant bunker under the market place, which would of course have been the end of them. Luckily good sense prevailed and they were beautifully restored. The Derbyshire Historic Buildings Trust, with which I was associated for many years, has had much success in saving small, desirable houses from the bulldozer. I hope that many of the stone barns that litter the Peak District may find a new role as night shelters for walkers. They are not the grand cathedral-like barns of the south of England, being often no more than sturdy sheds, but they are an important part of the landscape and many are falling to bits since they are no longer used for agricultural purposes.

The Bronze Age recumbent stones of Arbor Low on a high, bleak site near Youlgreave are worth a visit. I suggested to my sister Pam, who was deaf, that we should go there in the winter when the weekly *Dad's Army* television programme was at its most popular and she replied, 'Oh, Arthur Lowe, I should *so* much like to meet him.' Eyam is famous for its villagers' courageous behaviour. In 1665 a bundle of cloth contaminated by the plague arrived from London. To prevent the infection from spreading, Eyam's parson, the Reverend William Mompesson, persuaded the villagers not to leave. The deadly disease ravaged the small population but it was contained, and Mompesson and the villagers are honoured at an annual outdoor service held in the field where he preached while the disease was at its height.

Much of Derbyshire is Robin Hood country. Inn signs, plantations, a group of rocks near Elton and a big stone outcrop high up in the woods above the old park at Chatsworth carry his name. The legend is that Robin shot an arrow from this stony height, saying he would be buried where it fell. It reached Hathersage, eight miles away as the arrow flies, and although there is no sign of Robin Hood's grave, Little John is indeed buried in the churchyard. His grave was opened in the nineteenth century and a 32-inch-long thigh bone was found, which must have belonged to a man at least seven feet tall.

The immense oaks in the Old Park at Chatsworth are the outliers of Sherwood Forest and some are said to be a thousand years old. The oldest are kept alive by one or two small leafy branches. Their great hulks have rotted and become strange shapes, hollow and full of holes. They support an infinite variety of insect and bird life, and the younger and healthier trees provide big crops of acorns for the deer. We plant twenty or thirty in this part of the park every year and the fallen trees are never removed. Bracken gives the necessary privacy for the calves and fawns of the red and fallow deer.

No one can pretend that Derbyshire is famous for its food, though two delicacies are made in the county: Bakewell Pudding, a strange confection of almond paste, jam and pastry, and excellent Stilton cheese, which is made in a factory at Hartington.

The Peak District National Park was initiated in 1951 to look after some of the finest landscapes and villages. It takes no notice of county boundaries and wanders through parts of Cheshire and Staffordshire, though its main acreage is in Derbyshire. Although only 38,000 people live within the Peak Park, a third of the population of England is reckoned to live within an hour's drive of the Peak District. It is visited by millions of town dwellers from Manchester, Sheffield, Derby, Nottingham, Wolverhampton and Stoke, and the tourist industry is a valuable asset. In the most picturesque parts of the county, the landowners, farmers, smallholders and dwellers are constantly reminded of their heritage by the media, and it is to be hoped that this powerful lobby remembers that the villages will become Disneyland for trippers if they do not also recognise the need for jobs. If the county is to thrive, the limestone quarries, the mines for barites and fluorspar, and allied industries with their furnaces and factories, must go on as they have done for hundreds of years.

Derbyshire has more than its fair share of beautiful country. It also has some remarkable houses open to the public. In the south there is Sudbury Hall, home of the Vernons, which now belongs to the National Trust. Its somewhat forbidding exterior does not prepare you for the beauty of the plasterwork inside, described by Pevsner as 'luxuriant and breathtakingly skilful'. Near Derby are Kedleston Hall, Lord Curzon's Adam palace, and Melbourne Hall, with its splendid formal garden. Not far from Bakewell is Haddon Hall, that most English and romantic of Elizabethan buildings, and east of Chesterfield stands Hardwick Hall, Bess of Hardwick's surviving masterpiece, which never fails to astonish the visitor by the mysterious sweep of the staircase and the vast scale and beauty of the Presence Chamber and Long Gallery.

I leave home less and less often now but every time I return after a spell away, I am struck anew by this county's beauty – something I will never take for granted.

February 1982

LAGOPUS LAGOPUS SCOTICUS
AND ITS LODGERS

A delicacy unique to these islands is grouse. The grand restaurants in London, Paris and New York vie with each other to have the first and best birds on the menu for dinner on 12 August, the opening day of the grouse shooting season. Grouse moors are by their very nature high, wild and remote places. Such privacy is necessary for these elusive birds. No way of 'farming' or artificially rearing them has been devised. Grouse are mysterious even to the keepers who spend their lonely lives with them.

Like people, they are prone to disease. The biggest threat to these winged marvels is *Trichostrongylus tenuis*, or the Trichostrongyle worm, and attacks by these parasitic threadworms can be fatal. If they get the upper hand, the bird population can be wiped out and, instead of healthy broods, the moor is littered with skeletons. Shooting is a culling operation which prevents overpopulation, the cause of this and other diseases.

All ground-nesting birds, their eggs and chicks are at risk of being taken by foxes, weasels, stoats, rats and flying predators, including several species of hawks now protected by law. The weather at hatching time is crucial. A thunderstorm plus hail during the last two weeks of May can be catastrophic to the new chicks. They need warm weather to provide the minute insects on which they feed, until later when their diet consists of the tips of young heather, followed by the seed. The chicks grow at great speed, almost as quickly as broiler chicks turn into supermarket fare. By 12 August, the majority are only about twelve weeks old but even so they can fly like jets and are at their succulent best to eat.

I wonder if the people tucking into their dinners at the Connaught or the Ritz realise how many skilled professionals have made it possible for these birds to reach their tables. Gamekeepers; flankers with flags who guide the birds towards their fate; beaters who walk many miles through high heather and – worst of all – bracken, which on a wet day is no fun; gunsmiths from Spain to South Audley Street; cartridge manufacturers; the makers of Land Rovers and Argo Cats (machines on tracks that can go up the nearly perpendicular hills in Scotland); Mrs Barbour DBE and her coats; dog breeders and trainers; the 'guns' – the eight or so men who stand in the line of butts, on whose shooting prowess 'the bag' depends; pickers-up, the people whose dogs find the birds on the ground after the drive – all combine in a team effort, like an army manoeuvre, before a single bird is shot.

For all sorts of reasons, the uncertainty of the number that will fly over the butts is part of the charm of grouse shooting. Nothing can be guaranteed, least of all the weather. It is a question of First Shoot Your Grouse – not easy in a gale, with rain pelting into your face, hands numb with cold in spite of August on the calendar, or when it's so hot you can't bear to touch the metal on the Land Rover and the dogs drink enough water to float a ship. However, on a perfect day – when there's a breeze and sunny intervals, when the heather is full out and the pollen rising where the dogs hunt for fallen birds, when there's a clear view across the purple heights to the greener ground below – it is an earthly heaven. Or sometimes at Bolton Abbey, it can be raining hard on the tops and you suddenly catch a glimpse of the silver snake of the River Wharfe in its sunlit carved green valley and it is like a vision of the Promised Land.

Grouse fly high, they fly low (like winged rabbits), they

swoop, curve and jink, straight or twisting, singly, in pairs, or in packs of hundreds. They seem to be coming towards you and at the last moment they turn and cross the line three or four butts away. As you watch, disappointed, another bird comes at an impossible angle. You see it too late and a second chance is gone. A strong wind behind the birds increases their speed to a fly past; a wind against them and, hovering in the air almost stationary, they look easy but are as tricky as can be.

Getting the shot birds from the butts on the high ground of the Yorkshire or Perthshire moors to a road and thence to a motorway or an airport is, in itself, a challenge. When everything goes right and the birds arrive in the kitchens, they still have to be plucked, drawn and cooked before anyone who can afford it can eat them. The point of this saga is not just that grouse shooting is the most exciting and the most testing of sports but it also produces a harvest of valuable food.

Should you still be curious about these birds, I must refer you to a book which ought to have a place in every library, *The Grouse in Health and Disease*, Lord Lovat (ed.), 1911. With its accompanying appendix it weighs 7lb 7oz and is profusely illustrated with disgusting pictures of parasites, vastly enlarged ticks and the other lodgers that enjoy living a life of luxury in or on grouse. Perhaps the diners in London and Paris are aware of this but I would love to know if, poised with knife and fork, they have any idea that the expensive luxury they are about to eat can carry up to 10,000 worms, not to mention other parasites. The squeamish will be glad to hear that the worms are happy to live in the gut and so they've gone before the grouse reach the Sèvres plates.

Perhaps it is better not to know but just to enjoy the worms' host with no questions asked, and salute the dedication and skill of the keepers and the rest thanks to whom these epicurean treats have landed on your table.

WRITING A BOOK

Odd things happen when you write a book. The prospective publishers make out a contract – written in double Dutch of course, to confuse – couched in lawyers' language of 'The First Party', 'The Second Party', Marx Brothers' style. And no Sanity Clause. Suddenly the book turns into 'The Work', as in 'hereinafter termed the Work'. That's the first sensible thing they say. *Work* it jolly well is. (Just as *labour* is a brilliant description of having a baby – except that it ought to be called hard labour.)

Anyway, this Work is then the subject of a long rigmarole, beautifully printed on smart paper to make it seem less beastly. But in the middle of some unreadable paragraphs are sentences that strike an ice-cold note. For instance, there is talk about the Resolutions that will be passed if the publishers go into liquidation (which they will if they keep on taking books like mine) and the fate of the Author if he or she fails to deliver the Manuscript by a certain date. (He/she has to look sharp and pay for *everything* forthwith.)

Now I always thought of manuscripts as those immaculately written things on parchment, like Bess of Hardwick's accounts, with swirling, squiggling E's. Not at all, it just means a dreary old typed mess. Rather a relief, I must admit, because if one had to learn to write like Queen Elizabeth I on top of everything else it would be the giddy limit.

Then the publisher mentions something very worrying about what is going to happen to the books that go to the Philippines. Why this remote group of islands has to be singled out as a likely market and how the Filipinos could possibly be interested in the colour of curtains at Chatsworth, I really can't imagine, but I suppose Uncle Harold or someone knows.*

There is only one comforting bit in the whole of this lengthy document. It says, 'The Publishers shall not destroy any stock or sell it off as pulp without first informing the Author of their intention and offering the Author a few copies for personal use.' I think that's jolly nice of them. But what on earth is the author going to do with his few copies? He couldn't want to read them because he's written them. You can't eat them, take a taxi with them or plant them in the garden; you can't wear them or smoke them; they're no good as rat poison; you can't slate a roof with them or even make a decent garden seat. Never mind, it's a kind thought and one must be grateful for that. And so the contract maunders on to its incomprehensible legal conclusions.

The work part of the Work is very difficult to do with the telephone and other aspects of real life going on at home. So I took a room in a hotel by the sea for a few days. *Absolute failure.* The other denizens of the place took pity on an old woman holidaying alone and talked to me all through breakfast, lunch and dinner, both in the residents' lounge and in the darkest corner of the bar. So I took my exercise book to one of those glass-lined bus shelters you find on windswept English beaches, settled happily down, and lo and behold another lone woman came and sat beside me and started telling me about her dog. So I chucked it and went home. I only tell you all this in case you have the fancy to do the same yourselves one day. I think it's better to stick to farming and gardening, Agriculture and Horticulture.

The only thrilling part of all this is being paid for the twaddle you have written. A cheque arrives (the exact sum having been decided upon months ago so you had given up hope) and it looks really pleasing to the eye. But don't bank on it when you've banked it. Look again at the bit of paper and you'll see many a percentage deducted for one reason or another. VAT is mentioned and is horrid. Soon I expect VAT will be payable on VAT and so on, *ad infinitum*, till a minus sign wins the day. The final insult isn't, we have to admit, to do with publishers. It's the tax. And this almost makes the game not worth the candle. But it's all good clean fun. So out with the foolscap and on with a new one.

1982

* Deborah Devonshire's first book, *The House: A Portrait of Chatsworth*, published in 1982 by Macmillan, was commissioned by Harold Macmillan, Andrew Devonshire's uncle by marriage, who became chairman of his family's publishing firm after retiring from politics.

FLORA DOMESTICA: A HISTORY OF
FLOWER ARRANGING, 1500–1930
by Mary Rose Blacker

Flower arranging. Oh dear, I thought (having been to so many public functions where flowers are stuck sideways in their holder so the horizontal gladiolus stalks can't reach the water – a worrying style still practised in many a town hall). Never fear. This book is a wonder from start to finish. The author sees the subject with a scholar's eye and recounts the history of indoor fashion in flowers, from the sixteenth century until it reached a zenith of extravagance some hundred years ago.

It is said that cooks are prone to bad temper because their art is destroyed. The transitory nature of flower-arrangers is similar, but luckily for us it has been a subject beloved of artists over centuries and part of the fascination of this book lies in its illustrations. The familiar Dutch pictures of the seventeenth century, when it was cheaper to buy a painting of a tulip by an established artist than obtain a bulb of the precious plant itself, show glorious mixtures of flowers stuffed into containers of all kinds, including the incomparable blue-and-white Delftware brought to England by King William III's Mary. A few generations later, it's back to nature and we are exhorted by Batty Langley, the eighteenth-century Twickenham gardener, to make arrangements in a 'loose manner, so as not to represent a stiff bundle of flowers void of freedom'.

As more exotics arrived in this country, so did the variety of flowers grown in orangeries increase. In 1773, Horace Walpole

45

wrote from his Gothic fantasy, Strawberry Hill, 'My house is a bower of tuberoses.' The Sèvres factory in France and Wedgwood in England produced exquisite vases of all shapes and sizes to hold such wonders. Houses such as Osterley led the way with *garnitures* of up to thirteen pieces lined up on the mantelpiece. The National Trust has a band of volunteers at Osterley who recreate some of the eighteenth-century arrangements using flowers of the period, and that beautiful house is worthy of a visit for this reason alone.

Early nineteenth-century nurserymen, sniffing more business, began hiring out plants for receptions in the great London houses. Teams of gardeners were sent in to set them up and earned praise for their 'happy disposition' of plants at routs and fêtes. Sometimes the lady of the house did the job herself. There is a glorious description of the stout Duchess of Gordon in 1810, up a ladder, dressed in a dimity wrapper, 'knocking in nails to hold a garland of laurel over a picture', doing what 'she can get none of her awkward squad to do for her', before reappearing as hostess in 'the brightest spirits and the brightest diamonds'.

Soon palm trees appeared (at Chatsworth even banana trees). The gardeners and their 'decorators', as the arrangers were called, became increasingly ambitious until they went completely over the top and festooned everything, from chandeliers to plant boxes, in masses of flowers and leaves. 'Fences' of orchids and peonies erected along the tables made it impossible to see your fellow guests. Lady Monkwell, invited to dinner to meet Mr Gladstone, could only hear him for the hedge of peonies in the way. Lady Aberdeen scattered autumn leaves on her tablecloth. (They look like potato crisps but never mind, they were a change from ferns and carnations.) A monstrous innovation was the 'banded dish', a dining-table decoration that consisted of concentric circles of brilliantly coloured flowers arranged on a plate. There is an illustration of it from an American magazine of 1869 and it is the only ugly picture in the book, inexplicably chosen for the dust cover.

Hothouses proliferated in the gardens of big houses. At Waddesdon Manor, which had four acres under glass, a staggering variety of flowers was produced, including forests of Malmaison carnations that are notoriously difficult to grow. I am happy to say that they have appeared again at Waddesdon in profusion – an example of how everything at that house is done in slap-up style. The book is stuffed with anecdotes and reminders of the luxuries of times past. I shall have to go to Lyme Park to see the tobacco plants in the Bright Passage and to Polesden Lacy for a whiff of Mrs Ronnie Greville, that extravagant perfectionist.

My only criticism is of the illustrations of flowers in fireplaces. In our climate, fireplaces are for fires not flowers. The spirits sink on a cold June evening to see a bunch of roses where the welcoming glow ought to be. This is a tiny point in an otherwise perfect book. I hope Mrs Blacker will now tell us what happened to Floral Art from 1930–2000. She must.

July 2000

BOOK SIGNINGS AND LITERARY LUNCHES

Publishers sometimes think it is a Good Idea for an author to do a book signing to give their book a shove. The author is invited to a bookshop where an apparently inexhaustible supply of the wretched things is piled in heaps round Exhibit A, the author.

The staff in the bookshop are kindness itself. They have put a table and chair in the cave of books with familiar covers, so you feel at home. The signing has been advertised and it is a matter of pride to the staff, and terror to the author, to see if anyone turns up. When the appointed moment comes, the author settles in the chair, armed with pen and specs and, with luck, some would-be customers shuffle into view. Even if they have come on purpose to buy the book, they look at several identical volumes as if there might be a difference between one copy and another.

It is strange how few people seem to be buying the book for themselves. He/she picks one up, looks doubtfully at it, turns it round and says, 'It's for my mother, actually.' Younger customers say, 'It's for my grandmother, actually.' 'Oh, good,' says the author, 'that is really nice of you. What shall I write in it?' Long pause, while the buyer considers how the recipient should be addressed, as the author can't very well call someone else's mother/grandmother 'Mummy' or 'Granny'. So the Christian name is chosen. It has to be spelt out, especially if it happens to be Sheila, a trap with a good chance of 'gh' at the end. Luckily, the most usual name is Margaret and, as far as I know, there is no peculiar spelling there. But names get ever more unlikely and you have to listen carefully to the invented ones.

The next customer tells her life story. That's fine as long as there is no one behind her, but it can make the attention wander if you see one or two people who are obviously in a hurry and don't want to hear of far-off school days or a shared Oxfordshire childhood. Then comes a man, rolled umbrella if in Piccadilly, tweed coat and pale trousers if in Burford. 'Three copies? Oh thank you. What shall I put?' 'Just your signature, please.' Quickly done and off he goes. Obviously an excellent fellow, the sort the wireless calls a decision maker. Usually, the messages to be written are pretty ordinary. As yet, I have not had the one a famous author of my acquaintance told me about. A man formed up and asked nervously, 'Could you put "For Marlene – sorry about last night"?'

Bookshop regulars spot the chairs and the pile of identical books and dart in the opposite direction to avoid having to buy out of pity something they don't want. They ask, 'Where are the maps?' or 'Are there any books on beavers?' and make off like lightning.

With luck, the pile has diminished in the hour which has passed. So have the customers. Now you can have a good talk to the shop staff and find out what is really selling while you sign a few copies for stock. The devotion to books of the staff or owner of the shop, as the case may be, shines out and you come away wondering about the charm of the written word.

❦

A literary lunch is another matter. Three authors parade their wares by talking about them after two courses of so-called food for which people have actually paid. Usually there is not much literature on show because the books are 'popular' (or the lunch would be a failure). One of the speaker-authors tells doubtful stories in his allotted ten minutes, to the joy or embarrassment of the audience according to their taste. The other authors look at their watches, mindful of a train to catch. Eventually they all move to the tables where they are to sign and the rubbishy book disappears while the other two, over which the writers have taken real trouble, remain in their original piles, sadly slow to move.

At one of these entertainments I found myself in the company of Jeffrey Archer (before he was famous) and Arthur Marshall, who was indeed famous both for his inimitable radio perform-ances in which he would turn into the school matron and, more important, as a television star. His book roared away. He became a dear friend, the best company ever, and stayed with us at Chatsworth several times. One hot summer day we were walking across the big lawn crowded with people lying in heaps listening to the Sunday band. A woman spotted him: 'Is it?' I heard her say. 'It can't be . . . IT *IS!*' and round they came like bees to honey, for a word, a signed bit of paper, anything to remind them they had actually met the man who made them laugh.

I sometimes read about the other author at that strange Literary Lunch but I have never seen him since.

September 2007

THE TULIP
by *Anna Pavord*

From the dedication to Valerie Finnis, the acknowledged queen of English gardeners, this book is a rare treat. Taking as its subject a single genus of flower, it is written by a scholar and reads like a thriller.

There cannot be anyone who does not love tulips, if only because of the time of year of their flowering. If roses are synonymous with summer, tulips are the tangible evidence of spring. Of course we love them but we may not know that their story is as fascinating as the flowers themselves, with 'a background full of more mysterious dramas, dilemmas, disasters and triumphs than any besotted *aficionado* could reasonably expect'. It certainly is.

The native habitat of the tulip extends from Ankara to Tashkent and it was from Turkey that the first bulbs (or roots as they were called) came to Europe. In 1559, a Swiss botanist described seeing its 'gleaming red petals and its sensuous scent' in a Bavarian garden – the first known report of the flower in western Europe. The traders of the Dutch East India Company introduced it to Holland, where it soon became the object of 'tulipomania', and the madly desired flowers began to change hands for prices far above rubies. The usually stolid Dutch lost their heads over the striped, feathered and flamed flowers, that mysterious 'breaking' of colour which was caused by a virus. It was these flowers that commanded the wildest prices. The mania spread to France. At the height of the madness a man swapped his brewery for a single bulb. The crazy trade reached its zenith in 1637, when the inevitable crash came and trading was banned. Boom and bust is nothing new.

Protestant refugees fleeing religious persecution in Europe in the late sixteenth century took the valuable and easily carried bulbs to use as currency in their adopted countries, including England. They were soon taken up by nurserymen who supplied the owners of the formal gardens fashionable in the seventeenth century. The fancy spread quickly and amateur growers, known as 'florists', joined the tulip train and kept many of the choicest strains going throughout the eighteenth century. Clubs sprang up and tulip shows with attendant feasts were organised. By the 1820s, the rivalry between clubs in the north and the south of England was intense. Inter-club rows of mammoth proportions were commonplace and jealous rivals destroyed each other's tulip beds. At a Lancashire show, the finest entry (according to its owner) was stolen during dinner before it could be judged. Experts differed on standards of judging and views about the form of the blooms; insulting letters to horticultural journals flew to and fro. Judges had to be men of courage. The chapter on 'The Florist's Tulip' is comedy bordering on farce.

Of the many societies formed during the last century, only the Wakefield and North of England Tulip Society remains, where the blooms are shown in beer bottles as of yore. Tulips were the passion of artisans, and workers in the dark satanic mills fulfilled their artistic longings through the beauty of the flowers. The lack of a garden did not stop one engine driver in Derby – he grew his along the railway embankment.

The Tulip is too heavy to read in bed but once you have started there is no question of going to bed so it doesn't matter.

December 1998

UNSTEALABLES

The trouble about book thieves is that they don't see themselves as such. They borrow and forget with no criminal intent. But they pick the best without fail and leave a gap, unnoticed probably for months, and then you want the missing book for a quote, a story – or all of it – and it's gone.

I seldom read for pleasure but every now and then something takes my fancy and I mind so much when I've finished that, like my father, I can't bear the thought of beginning another. In an effort to keep my loved ones, I have got them penned, as it were, in my bedroom. The hard core is by friends and family, from grandfathers to children, and some of them have lost their spines in the rough and tumble of life in a hanging bookcase. They are all precious, of course, but too many to go into here. They include *Park Top: A Romance of the Turf* by Andrew Devonshire, a book that reveals as much about its author as it does about the famous filly, bought for him as a bargain yearling in 1965 by his friend and trainer, Bernard van Cutsem. And there's *A Fine Old Conflict* by Jessica Mitford. When she was working on this autobiographical book, I asked my sister what its title was to be. 'The Final Conflict', she replied. I wasn't listening properly and thought she said 'A Fine Old Conflict', which is what she decided on.

The others are a motley lot and all prized. I made a list of a few some years ago: *Fowls and Geese and How to Keep Them*; *Book* by Lady Clodagh Anson and *Another Book* by the same author;

What Shall We Have Today? by X. Marcel Boulestin; Priscilla Napier's autobiography, *A Late Beginner*; *Another World*, the first twenty years of Anthony Eden's life; *The Secret Orchard of Roger Ackerley* by Diana Petre; *The Prince, the Showgirl and Me* by Colin Clark; *Rio Grande's Last Race and Other Verses* by A. B. Peterson; *The Best of Beachcomber*; Thomas Hardy's *The Woodlanders*; *The Anatomy of Dessert* (1933) by Edward A. Bunyard; *The Curse of the Wise Woman* by Lord Dunsany; *Peter Rabbit*; *Ginger and Pickles*; *Small is Beautiful* by E. F. Schumacher, and Peter Guralnick's *Last Train to Memphis: The Rise of Elvis Presley*.

There are also the essentials: *The Definitive Edition of Rudyard Kipling's Verse*; *The Collected Poems* of A. E. Housman and *The Oxford Book of English Verse* (1922 edition). The latter is inscribed 'Unity Mitford from Uncle George, Asthall, August 1925', with '11 years old' added in childish writing. Some years later, Unity wrote in it again, 'U.V.M., St. Margaret's, Bushey' – the school she loved and from which she was sacked. Since my sister's death, this volume, printed on India paper, has been my travelling companion. 'Lament of the Irish Immigrant' by Helen Selina, Lady Dufferin, which brings tears to this day, has been eliminated from later editions. Why?

The list has inevitably grown over the years; new ones have joined my classic crowd and more shelves have been filled.

Black Diamonds by Catherine Bailey is now next to *White Mischief* by James Fox.

The Day of Reckoning by Mary Clive. Born Pakenham, and still alive at 101, she is as good a story-teller as any of that tribe of writers. She writes of the 'day-to-day surroundings of well-to-do families' in the early part of the twentieth century. The illustrations, some familiar – *When Did You Last See Your Father?*, *The Finest View in Europe*, a cover of *Chatterbox* – others of private and national events, whirl you through her life with nostalgia and joy. But don't miss the text.

Ask the Fellows Who Cut the Hay by George Ewart Evans

(1909–88) is one of a cherished series that includes *Where Beards Wag All* and *The Horse in the Furrow*. The author describes rural life in Suffolk and set about his task just in time, when there were still farm labourers who could remember working the heavy soil with Suffolk horses and all that went with it.

Notes from a Small Island. The brilliant American Bill Bryson notices so much about this country which we take for granted but are fascinated to see described as new. It beats me why he is so fond of England and its natives – it's amazing that he stayed here after arriving on a foggy midnight in Folkestone to the typical English opposite of a welcome.

I galloped through *On the Black Hill* when it came out in 1982 in order to get an impression of Bruce Chatwin's inimitable way of writing, which carries you with him to the novel's inevitable tragic end.

Heinrich Hoffmann's *Struwwelpeter*, a terrifying illustrated book for children, could not find a publisher now. My sisters and I used to think that great Agrippa, 'foaming with rage in his dressing gown' and 'so tall, he almost touched the sky', was the double of my father.

Somerville and Ross: The World of the Irish R.M. by Lewis Gifford is a biography of my Anglo-Irish heroines who wrote about life in southernmost Ireland before the boom when there was only bust.

Coke of Norfolk and His Friends by A. M. W. Sterling was a Christmas present long ago from my Uncle Jack Mitford, who could not have guessed that agriculture would be my overriding interest.

They're Away was a present to Andrew from a bookmaker. It is my favourite volume of poetry about hunting and racing, by Beatrice Holden (1886–1968), a redoubtable hunting woman of Atherstone and Warwickshire fame. Years ago I stuck her obituary from *Horse & Hound* inside the cover. It ends, 'Gallop on blithe spirit, and may you find your heaven in a good grass country.' 'A Closing Memory of Lord Harrington' is one of her best, a mysterious tale known by all hunting people. Lord Harrington's dying wish was that his hounds should meet the day after his funeral. They quickly found a fox that ran straight to their master's grave, where 'the grass was trampled and pressed / Where yesterday the best-loved man in the Midlands was laid to rest'. The huntsman took off his cap and whispered, 'Gentlemen, I am taking them Home; / His Lordship has called his Hounds.'

Primrose McConnell's *Agricultural Note-Book* (1919 edition) is inscribed, 'After my death this book is to be given to Debo. With love Conrad Russell, XII Night 1947'. The blue-eyed Somerset dairy farmer became a friend during the war when Andrew was stationed at Warminster. He made cheese, and was as clever and individual as Russells are apt to be.

Primrose was a man. His *Note-Book* is dedicated to the memory of his son, also Primrose, who was killed in the Great War. It is closely packed with facts and figures pertaining to the land. The physical work expected of a farm labourer earning pitiful wages is shocking to us now. A man was expected to pitch 4,000 to 5,000 sheaves of corn a day and a woman to milk ten cows, night and morning, for 1¼d per cow.

Out of Africa by Karen Blixen. I suppose this book is on everyone's list.

If Hopes Were Dupes (1966) by 'Catherine York'. This is by my first cousin, Ann Farrer, who wrote this sorrowful account of her nervous breakdown and total dependence on her psychoanalyst. It would send a shiver down any spine.

The Uncommon Reader by Alan Bennett. How did he do it? I wish I knew. There are copies of this book all over the house. They won't last long. My own is guarded by fatter volumes, several inches thick (*Farm Live Stock of Great Britain* and *Mrs Beeton's Book of Household Management*), which protect this little jewel.

May God preserve them all.

JOHN FOWLER: PRINCE OF DECORATORS
by Martin Wood

It is not given to many for their surname to be turned into an adjective immediately recognisable by a section of society. 'Fowlerised' meant a house transformed by John Fowler to his (and the owner's) taste. In spite of having known John for many years, I had little idea of the extent of his work and influence until I read this book. Dedicated to looking and learning, he dealt with all dates and styles of buildings through scholarship and a prodigious memory.

He was born in 1906, a one-off in an unartistic family, with talents that took him to painting furniture for Peter Jones in 1934, where he earned £4 a week. He was refused a rise in wages so he and his colleagues downed paintbrushes and set up on their own.

They struggled on until 1938, when John joined Lady Colefax. Twice his age and a fashionable decorator with a shop in Mayfair, Sybil Colefax knew the women who wanted something more than Syrie Maugham's everlasting white and mushroom, which had ruled during the early 1930s. Fashion had moved on in its inexorable way and John seized the opportunity. Through his personality and knowledge he soon became the clients' favourite. He was exempted from war service because of myopia. While fabrics were rationed, he used his ingenuity to cover sofas with old curtains, and his clients' unwanted evening dresses were cut up to make trimmings or cushion covers.

In 1944, when Nancy Tree bought into the business now called Colefax & Fowler, she and John became an irresistible force. They bickered and sparred, they flounced out and flounced back, they laughed and got angry, and through this exhausting process produced some of the most beautiful interiors in the land. They fed off each other to the benefit of their clients. The business prospered through word of mouth: Nancy's friends and relations, who happened to be the highest echelons of society, aspired to this resourceful duo. Nancy had the ideas and taught John how the famous houses were to be lived in and enjoyed through comfort and beauty. John, the dictator of the work-room, got on and performed the task, supported by his skilled craftsmen. He taught them as Nancy had taught him.

Before John came on the scene, Nancy and her husband Ronnie Tree had bought Ditchley Park, a James Gibbs house in Oxfordshire, and made it an earthly paradise. Ditchley was an inspiration to John. In 1954 Nancy (now married to Jubie Lancaster) restored Haseley Court, near Oxford, where their full-blown taste reached its zenith. The list of places John worked on reads like a dictionary of that unique English asset envied by the rest of the world – the country house. It included Blithfield Hall in Staffordshire, Radburne Hall near Derby, Mereworth Castle in Kent, Arundel Park and Syon House. Most were private houses but some opened to the public after the war. The book's index shows hardly a county without an example of his work.

In 1956 John got his first job with the National Trust at magical Claydon House in Buckinghamshire. This led to many more, including Sudbury Hall in Derbyshire. I was on the committee for its redecoration before the Trust opened it to the public. I carried John's patterns, flew up and down stairs, moved furniture ('Don't push that chair – PICK IT UP') and trudged the length of the Long Gallery time after time at his bidding. He was already mortally ill but did not spare himself or his helpers in the cold, unwelcoming rooms that turned into fairyland under his direction. His treatment of the staircase was an example of his disdain for democracy. The committee arrived one day to find that the carved balusters had been painted white and the walls a brilliant yellow. Jaws dropped, but the murmuring went unheeded and we moved on to the next thing.

Cornbury Park and Chequers, two mammoth jobs, were his last major commissions. Neither is accessible to you and me but both are mighty impressive according to the lucky few who know them.

John was two people. A tyrant to his staff, he changed into a delightful companion after work, amusing and amused. He took to gardening and saw the importance of the relationship between indoors and out. He was also a master of scale. The photographs in the book of a 'pocket' flat, the size of a double garage, give the impression of a much bigger place. He dealt with palaces and cottages with equal enthusiasm.

This book is an historic document, a reminder of times past, beautifully written with photographs that accurately depict the interiors – even the colours are right. It will be the standard reference book of taste in England during the second half of the twentieth century.

December 2007

TIARAS

What are tiaras for? They are the finishing flourish to the best evening dress, accompanied by long white gloves of thinnest suede, ending above the elbow and cleaned after every outing. They are the night-time equivalent of an Ascot hat, the female accompaniment to a man's white tie and decorations, the opposite of dressing down and the pinnacle of the jeweller's art. They are often accompanied by necklaces and brooches of a like design, a casket of delight with which to decorate a female form.

Before the last war, tiaras were worn by married women (only) at all the grand balls in London, and very beautiful they were. Some of the most striking were once-seen-never-forgotten. The face underneath was known by the helmet of diamonds, rubies, emeralds, sapphires and pearls glittering above: harsh, spiky and upstanding, or a humbler circlet threaded through the marcel waves of the hair. It was like recognising people in a country crowd by their dogs. We would have been very muddled if there had been a general swap around and the Duchess of Northumberland wore Lady Astor's and Lady Londonderry turned up in one of the Duchess of Buccleuch's. Some of the young women were fairylike in their beauty. The old and fat were not, but even they were improved by their headdresses.

The royal tiaras, some of extraordinary splendour, are familiar through being much photographed, but family jewels of lesser mortals are left in the bank and seldom given an airing. Like most

English heirlooms, the jewels belong to the man and are worn by the wives. (If things go on as they are, I see the day looming when it will be the other way round.) These women are usually too busy looking after difficult husbands and animals to bother about having their diamonds cleaned, so the royal jewels shine out, always in pristine order, and the enormous stones worn by the peeresses, happier in gumboots and strangers to the hair-dresser, are apt to look dim in comparison.

Queen Mary wore tiaras like she wore her toques – as if they were part of her being. In her day, when formality and rigid standards of dress were the rule, King George wore a tailcoat, white tie and the blue riband of the Garter while Queen Mary wore an evening dress and tiara, even when they were dining alone. A favourite was a diamond bandeau, the base of a tiara given to her as a wedding present in 1893 by 'The Girls of Great Britain and Ireland'.

My grandmother-in-law, Evelyn Duchess of Devonshire, was Mistress of the Robes to Queen Mary for forty-three years from 1910. Together they weathered long hours of tiara'd evenings, including those during the fabulous Indian Durbar in Delhi in 1911. The magically beautiful but relentless programme, carried out in torrid heat, was exhausting for all concerned, and after one particularly lengthy evening Granny Evie was heard to say, 'The Queen has been complaining about the weight of her tiara . . . *The Queen doesn't know what a heavy tiara is.*'

Evelyn knew what she was talking about. The larger of the two Devonshire diamond tiaras is indeed a whopper. It was made in 1893 for Louise, the 8th Duke of Devonshire's wife. She was formerly married to the Duke of Manchester and was known as the 'Double Duchess'. The diamonds have an historic interest. They were not, like so many, bought by their owner as a result of the fall of various royal houses; they came from the Devonshire Parure. This set consists of seven monumental pieces of jewel-lery, which, until you look closely at them, might have been pulled out of the dressing-up box. They are a bizarre combination of antique (Greek and Roman) and Renaissance cameos and intaglios carved from emeralds, rubies, sapphires and semi-precious stones – cornelian, onyx, amethysts and garnets – set in gold and enamel of exquisite workmanship by C. F. Hancock of London. They were commissioned by the dear old, extravagant 6th Duke of Devonshire, the 'Bachelor' Duke, for his niece, Countess Granville, to wear at the coronation of Tsar Alexander II in Moscow in 1856. This tiara and its companion necklace, stomacher and bracelet are very prickly to wear. I know because I put them all on for a Women's Institute performance when I was cast as 'The Oldest Miss World in the World'.

My mother-in-law, Mary Devonshire, was Mistress of the Robes to the Queen from 1953 to 1967. Tall and beautiful, she looked magnificent when dressed for a grand occasion. The big tiara suited her perfectly and anyone who saw her in close attendance on the young Queen at the coronation in 1953 will remember the perfection of her bearing on that famous day. In the course of her duties, which included formal banquets for visiting heads of state and other ceremonial occasions, she used to fetch the jewels from the bank stowed in a Marks & Spencer carrier bag.

There can be no slouching with a tiara on your head. It makes you stand and sit up straight. In spite of combs, hairpins and kirby grips, there is always the possibility of it slipping, which makes the most dedicated teetotaller look the worse for wear. Tiaras elevate the wearer, making her look more distinguished and taller because of the unaccustomed posture (which used to be taught as 'deportment', long forgotten in this sloppy age).

The Queen Mother was a lesson to us all in this. She was not tall but her carriage was such that she would have been outstanding in a crowd even if she were not a queen. When she was over eighty, I remember seeing her sit bolt upright through an entire performance of the ballet at Covent Garden, her back never touching her chair.

Tiaras could often be 'taken down', unscrewed from their frames by miniature carpenter's tools, and fastenings screwed on to the back to make brooches. These were the ruin of many an evening dress when the pin was blunt and had to be forced through satin or silk, leaving a sizeable hole.

In the 1930s, the 6th Duke of Portland was wounded by the enormous diamond headdress about to be worn by his beautiful wife, Winnie. He went to talk to her when she was getting dressed and sat on a nearby chair. The tiara was there first and he leapt up, impaled on the platinum spikes that held the precious stones. It was hopelessly broken. 'Oh never mind,' said Winnie, not bothering about her husband's injured behind, 'I'll wear another one.' Some could be useful weapons. Two quarrelling women sprouting branched spears on their heads look for all the world like stags about to clash antlers in the October rut. A curiosity of about 1860 is a coronet of fox's teeth, mounted points upward. It belongs to the Marquess of Waterford, an Irish peer whose family has always been devoted to foxhunting. Lady Waterford tells me it is not often worn.

At a big dance in the 1950s and 1960s it was not uncommon for men to wear tailcoats and women their jewels. I remember going to such an entertainment in London in the early 1960s, by myself as Andrew had an engagement elsewhere. With unwonted confidence I wore the big tiara. It must have looked rather odd because my home-made dress of cotton broderie anglaise was definitely not up to it. When I ran out of partners and wanted to go home, I went out to look for a taxi. It never occurred to me that it might not be a good idea to stand alone in the street, long after midnight, with a load of diamonds round my neck and 1,900 more glittering above my head.

One memorable evening we were staying at Windsor Castle for a dance given by the Queen. I came down to dinner, got-up as I thought our hostess and the other guests would be, the big tiara firmly in place. To my horror none of the other women wore theirs. It is far worse to be overdressed than underdressed and I sat through dinner wishing I was anywhere else. When the dancing began, I took it off, put it under a chair and enjoyed myself enormously. I suppose Windsor Castle is the only house where you could be sure of finding the blessed thing still there at bedtime.

March 2002

AUCTION CATALOGUES

The catalogues of the big auction houses arrive here by post. They are fat and heavy and when you have flicked over the pages that tell you how to bid and how to pay (and your fate if you don't pay pronto) you reach the nub of the matter, profusely illustrated, with what you are encouraged to buy.

The number and quality of works of art that find their way to the salerooms never cease to amaze me. In spite of the vast quantity now frozen to death in galleries and museums, a big proportion of which is not shown because there is no room, a seemingly endless supply still passes through the auction houses of London, Paris, New York and Geneva – covering the whole gamut of artists and craftsmen from over the centuries.

The scholarship and meticulous research that make up the descriptions in these catalogues are a history lesson in themselves, as well as a lesson in the history of art. Specialists in each subject trot out their expertise. Details of works by familiar and unfamiliar names sometimes end with 'Thanks to . . . for the identification of the sitter' or 'Thanks to . . . for confirmation of the artist'. In these cases even the experts, in their ceaseless search for accuracy, have had to call on others for help. But suddenly your unquestioning acceptance of all this scholarly stuff, the last word in some narrow field of painting or other art, is nullified by the ignorance of much to do with birds, fruit and flowers, crops in landscapes, beasts of the field, horses, carriages, hounds and dogs.

Sporting art may be in fashion but cataloguers are often wide of the mark. They ought to be sentenced to a few months in the country before being let loose on their job. When you think of the teams of young people employed by auction houses, who are often brought up in the shires – by followers of hounds, keen shots, farmers, foresters, fishermen and gardeners – the direct-ors would do well to ask these boys and girls to get their dads to cast a critical eye over the descriptions of forthcoming sales. This would avoid partridges being described as grouse, grouse as black game, snipe as woodcock, ptarmigan (even in white winter plumage) as grouse, hares as rabbits and vice versa. Beagles, har-riers and foxhounds would no longer be muddled up. Haycocks would not be described as *corn stooks*, or haymaking as *harvesting corn*. The Scottish illustrator, Archibald Thorburn, who knew one bird from the other, wouldn't allow these untutored descrip-tions, so when his works are on offer they are correctly named – by the artist.

Some artists, however, are apt to muddle us. *On a Mossy Bank* may combine birds' nests and all sorts of flowers as though by chance. This is where we need a resident botanist to stop prim-roses being described as cowslips and an RSPB officer to stop the artists pulling nests and eggs from where they belong and dropping them in the open. The enormous canvases of Dutch flower-painters depict unseasonal combinations of tulips and roses, daffodils and passion flowers, hyacinths and dahlias, which is confusing. Did they paint the spring flowers and leave gaps till the summer ones came along? I wish I knew.

I have a sneaking feeling that when it comes to less important pictures, cataloguers may have an off-the-peg list of descriptions to fit. The figures in rural scenes are always *Peasants* or *Cottagers*. If the female peasants have got pots on their heads they will be *In an Italianate Landscape*. Any water in the way puts them into *A River Landscape*. If you can see for miles, start with *An Extensive Landscape*. Should there be a glimpse of the sea it will be *A Coastal*

Landscape or perhaps *A Rocky Coastal Landscape*. Sometimes add *With a Town Beyond* or *With a Storm Raging* or *With a Tavern*. Peasants and cottagers *carouse* outside these taverns, they are seldom just plain drinking. Cottagers' wives are quiet types who are *Gathering Flowers* or *Knitting* – especially *In a Cottage Interior* where there is a wooden cradle in front of the fire, a sheepdog lying on a home-made rag rug and Grandpa sitting in a rocking chair smoking a clay pipe.

Faggot Gatherers make up a considerable part of the rural population, and their near-relations, *Woodcutters*, provide fuel for the *Charcoal Burners in a Clearing*, who make a great deal of smoke – now illegal. These law-breakers seem to be very decent sorts of criminals, so it is just as well they are no more as I don't think they would take kindly to being shut up in prison.

Returning to sport, a favourite subject is *Ferreting* – sometimes threatened by *A Gathering Storm*. *Ratting* is the lowest of the low and unaffected by the weather. Anglers seem to be a better class of sportsmen as they cast their lines *On a River in a Wooded Landscape*. Fishermen spend a lot of time telling stories to audiences of little boys sitting on a breakwater gazing at the catch. Highland cattle and red deer are unheeding of the snow *In a Highland Landscape*. But the ubiquitous *Faggot Gatherers* are often bent double against a bitter wind as they approach their thatched cottages where, presumably, the faggots will be burnt in an attempt to warm the knitting wife, the baby and its grandfather.

At a meet of hounds all the followers are described as *huntsmen*. As every country skoolboy knows there is only one huntsman, so this is a serious mistake. When it comes to horses the cataloguers prefer chestnut to any other colour, so bays, browns and blacks are *chestnuts*. Anything as unusual as a strawberry roan stumps them; piebald and skewbald are reversed, and as for a flea-bitten grey, such a rarefied description is far beyond them. Shire horses hauling timber wagons are mistaken for Clydesdales. *Cavalry*

Charging is often just the King's Troop practising their act for an agricultural show.

This very day a catalogue has come from one of the leading auction houses. *A Thoroughbred Mare and her Foal* – the foal, as any fool can see, is an old Shetland pony. Dogs and hounds get the same treatment. An obvious Spaniel is a Setter while a Great Dane turns into an Irish Wolfhound, as does a Deer Hound. West Highland Whites are in fashion so they are correctly described, but Cairns are Scotties.

None of these yawning gaps in the knowledge of country affairs seems to matter. Beauty is in the eye of the beholding bidders, who cheerfully pay millions of pounds for their fancy.

Contemporary art is another subject altogether. The creators of these strange daubs have given up and *Untitled* is often as far as they will go – a wise decision.

There is one more twist to the ways of auctioneers. In the name of economy, two have written to me recently to say they cannot go on supplying catalogues for nothing. No wonder, when they must cost a fortune to produce. So I wrote back to thank them for past generosity and to say how much I have appreciated receiving them over the years. The surprising result is that I now receive two copies of each. I'm not complaining but it is a funny way to economise.

BUYING CLOTHES

London is becoming very odd. Shops, in particular. Wandering round the environs of Sloane Street, I saw in a window the very garment for the coming Derbyshire winter – a woolly coat one degree up from an old woman's cardigan, decent to look at and warm. So I went in, looked closer and still fancied it.

I asked the very nice but not exactly what the prime minister would call a British shop girl in a British job (sorry, Customer Service Assistant), just what colour it was. The reason for this basic question is that I have got an eye disease which muddles colours. The C.S.A. looked doubtfully at it, read a label or two and cleverly found the answer, saying very slowly, 'ELM'.

For one who cannot distinguish colours this is not very helpful. First of all, we have – alas – been denied the sight of an elm since the 1960s when they all died. The majority of shoppers are too young to remember them but depending on the time of year they were three totally different colours: in spring the buds were brownish-pink, in summer the leaves were dark green and in autumn they turned into the purest and most beautiful yellow.

I bought the coat but I have no idea if it is pink, green or yellow. What's more, I have suddenly thought, was it the *bark* they were on about? Add silvery dark-brown with deep fissures as a fourth possibility. I would love to meet the manufacturer's colour expert and try to pin her down.

THE DUCHESS OF DEVONSHIRE'S BALL,
1897

A fancy-dress ball lasts only a few hours. Compared with other occasions for dressing up – performing in plays, ballets, operas and so forth – which are often repeated night after night, a ball is as ephemeral as a dream. Yet once they have accepted the invitation, serious grown-up people will take endless trouble – and often suffer extreme discomfort – to appear on the one-and-only night as their chosen character. The enthusiasm is infectious and the grumbling about what a bother it all is soon forgotten in the spirit of competition that goads the guests into making sure that their clothes are more beautiful, authentic, outrageous or funny than their neighbours'.

The Devonshire House fancy-dress ball held on 2 July 1897 to honour Queen Victoria's Diamond Jubilee is legendary. Until my daughter Sophy began to find out more about it for her book, *The Duchess of Devonshire's Ball*, I thought that, like many legends, it had become ridiculously exaggerated over the years. I was wrong.

In the days when a ball was given in London on four or five nights a week in May, June and July, when the now-vanished private houses of Mayfair and Kensington were going full blast, it had to be a very special entertainment to arouse much interest. The Duchess of Devonshire's ball was a very special entertainment.

It was not difficult for Louise Duchess to mobilise her female guests – they can have had little else to do but arrange themselves for such an occasion and one can easily picture the excitement and pleasure it gave. But even clever old Louise must have been surprised at managing to persuade a lot of middle-aged men to order their costumes and suffer the tedium of trying them on.

That she was able to persuade her sixty-four-year-old husband to give the party in the first place shows how indulgent he was towards her. At the time, the duke was Lord President of the Council, responsible for education and the Cabinet's defence committee in Lord Salisbury's third government. By this time he had given up frivolity and his idea of a pleasurable evening was a game of bridge with his wife and some old friends. One can only imagine how he must have groaned and sighed at the prospect of the night's entertainment. But he entered into the spirit of the thing to please his adored Louise.

Perhaps Englishmen secretly love dressing up. Perhaps, by pretending to be somebody else, they lose the self-consciousness with which so many of them are plagued. Certainly at any ceremonial occasion, whether military, ecclesiastic, academic or political, whether in the City of London or at Westminster, it is the men who wear fancy dress. They appear in cock feathers and sables, ermine and swords, lace and silk tights, and even carry posies of flowers through the streets, while their women melt into the surroundings like hen pheasants in the bracken.

Luckily for posterity, the duchess's guests submitted to the boredom of being photographed for a privately printed album presented to Louise by her friends. The expressionless faces of the subjects remind us of the long exposures necessary for photography a hundred years ago. Fashion in beauty has changed and looking at the photographs of the women (with a few glittering exceptions like the Duchesses of Portland and Marlborough), it is hard to imagine the sitters as the heart-breakers they certainly were. One could be forgiven for questioning if they even possessed a heart, or any other organ for that matter, as they seem to be made of wood or some harder material, standing set as concrete against the photographer's backcloths.

In spite of the rooms full of papers at Chatsworth, there is surprisingly little about Devonshire House itself. Rebuilt in 1733 after a fire, to designs by William Kent, it stood opposite the Ritz Hotel in Piccadilly. The 9th Duke of Devonshire sold it in 1919 but reserved some of the fixtures and fittings. Five years later it was pulled down by its new owners. Some of the doors (the ones from the billiard room had removable panels to let the smoke out) and fireplaces were used at Birch Grove, Harold Macmillan's house in Sussex. Harold's wife, born Dorothy Cavendish, was a daughter of the 9th Duke and had lived at Devonshire House as a child. For years, much of the furniture and even the silk off the walls were spread about Chatsworth. Piled high in the kitchen-maids' bedrooms were silk curtains, cushions, tassels and braids. Chimneypieces lay on their backs in the forge by the stables, while in the granary loft above were stored the London state harness of the carriage horses, extravagantly carved and painted pelmets, gilded fillets, and other grubby and tattered remains of old glory.

Just before Devonshire House was sold someone took a pho-tograph of Billy Hartington, my brother-in-law, on the staircase. He was two years old at the time and stood on the wide shallow steps at the curve of the staircase with its crystal handrail that led to the saloon and other reception rooms. The photograph is doubly sad: the house disappeared in a pile of dust and twenty years later Billy was killed in action. The destruction of the house is one of many such tragedies of the twentieth century and it is not much comfort to think that today it would be forbidden to pull it down. The palace on Piccadilly has gone for ever and with it the elegance of the ghosts of 1897 whose everyday clothes are fancy dress now.

1985

A LONDON RESTAURANT ON TRIAL

One of the perks of being a director of a hotel is visiting and eating at the competition. The idea is to taste, look and learn. On this mission (and on the instructions of our chairman) the managing director of the Devonshire Arms Country House Hotel at Bolton Abbey, Yorkshire, and I met for lunch at one of the most famous restaurants in London. The Devonshire Arms is the proud possessor of a Michelin star, so the managing director and his chef know a thing or two about the job.

As I seldom go to London, it is an excitement to see what's what in the fashionable world. I have known the chosen restaurant* for many years but I am so stuck in my ways that I was surprised by the changes I found since last eating there. There is a black-trouser-clad lady greeter, a new role in the restaurant staff. She was one of the few females to be seen, as the place soon filled up with men – a good omen for the quality of the food (and bad for the size of the bill).

The arrangement of the tables is ideal, like a railway carriage with high divisions, so the booming voices of the confident customers discussing business and sport are contained. The decor is brown, beige and more brown. No colour. The lighting is perfect – full marks for that, as it is the hardest thing to get right. The plates are a normal size, none of those huge oval platters like dog dishes that put you off eating.

Every table was taken. The charming head waiter (French?

Italian?) answered our questions very politely. How many covers? Is there a private room? He may have smelt a rat and imagined we were from one of the many magazines that describe places to eat, or perhaps he just thought we were naturally curious country-bumpkins on an outing. My companion and I considered the overheads as we watched the young, long-legged waiters, so numerous that they were in danger of running into each other. These boys have taken the place of the middle-aged women in white overalls, with a lot of nanny about them, who used to serve the excellent, plain English nursery food in a plain English nursery way. Bread-and-butter pudding and raspberry crumble came naturally to them, as they do to the customers, all brought up on such no-frills fare. I am sorry the nannies have turned into waiters but that is because second childhood is setting in.

When the bill came my companion and I smiled and marvelled at the prosperity of this country. Stuffed with decent food, one glass of house wine and two glasses of fizzy water, we went home to write our reports for the chairman. I can't wait for the next outing.

February 2004

* Wilton's in Jermyn Street.

EDENSOR POST OFFICE

They shut our post office yesterday. For the first time in living memory there is no early morning light at that end of the ancient cottage and the little shop that goes with it. The stacks of newspapers and magazines with unlikely titles have disappeared overnight.

No longer can a letter be weighed to go to the ends of the earth. No more postmaster, one elbow on the counter, turning the thick cardboard sheets with brightly coloured stamps of all prices lurking between them, painstakingly adding them up to the right amount for a letter to Easter Island or Nizhni Novgorod. No more blue airmail stickers to speed the thing along like a migrating bird. The letter box remains, but what good is that without a stamp? It is a ghostly reminder that yet another service in another part of life is finished.

So it is into the car once more to queue in the Bakewell supermarket instead of walking down the hill, looking at the gardens and their dogs, and seeing the minibus calling for the schoolchildren. What about the old people who haven't got a car? What about the other pensioners in the village? No one cares about them because they don't stab each other after a bout of drinking and have never bothered the police or a counsellor in their long lives. They are just the nostalgic past because they behave decently. For these people, who spend most of their time alone at home, the post office was like a club. Old and young met there, people called in on their way to work to pick up a paper, as well as children on their way to and from school. They had a chat, a grumble, compared gardening notes or gave news of a former resident who has gone to New Zealand. We all knew each other, we knew when someone was ill or had gone on holiday. Now our meeting place is dark and dead.

The government don't care. They pretend to be keen on 'rural welfare'. They have invented 'community centres' and spend our money building monstrous new ones when our post office *was* one. A vital support, impossible to value in money but sticking out a mile to those of us who live in villages, has gone. Teas in the cottage remain popular but the locals don't go out to tea – they have it in their own home. Fine-weather walkers and tourists are welcome but they don't belong, their roots are elsewhere.

There has been a post office in Edensor since 1886. It was one of the first in a small village, presumably provided to serve Chatsworth. By 1892 the postmistress, Mrs Jane Bacon, dealt with two deliveries and two collections on weekdays and one of each on Sundays. The then Duke of Devonshire and his politician guests made good use of the newly installed telegraph office and the locals appreciated several other services.

A bellboy, aged twelve and a half, was the human on whom Chatsworth relied for telegrams. One of his jobs was to run the half mile to the Edensor post office to fetch and send them. His name was W. K. Shimwell. This education served him far better than sitting in a classroom, as he went on to be private secretary to the duke when he was governor-general of Canada, 1916–21, and later became comptroller of Chatsworth and clerk of works to all the buildings scattered over the thousands of acres of the Derbyshire estate, including Chatsworth itself. Sometimes it pays to leave school early.

It's all gone. There is no bellboy and no post office. Now, that horrible form of communication, email, rules. Even people in the same office send emails to each other instead of talking.

Bang go human relationships. All is sacrificed to speed. No time to ponder – bung off the email and back comes another in a ridiculous new language invented for it. With no proper signature, no envelope for privacy and paper galore, manners, spelling and grammar are out of the window. Email is cold, impersonal, demanding, unfading, invading and often incomprehensible. Like the hymn, it is immortal, invisible . . . and silent as light.

April 2008

THE ARRIVAL OF THE KENNEDYS IN
LONDON, 1938

'Coming out' had a different meaning in 1938 from what it has today. The last London season before the Second World War followed much the same pattern as it had done before the First.

For a small section of people there were three frantic months of entertainments. For eighteen-year-old girls and their young men-friends there was a coming-out dance (and sometimes two) four nights a week, and often one in the country on a Friday night (not on Saturdays, because it was not seemly to dance into Sunday morning) from early May till the end of July. The bands, led by Ambrose, Carroll Gibbons and, best of all, Harry Roy, played all night every night for our pleasure.

We took this strange state of affairs for granted; it was part of life, to be enjoyed or endured according to temperament. There were country weekend parties in the houses of debutantes' parents, race meetings – from Ascot and Goodwood to the local point-to-point – topped up in August by Highland gatherings, which included the jolliest and rowdiest of reel parties.

1938 was a vintage year for beautiful girls. Hollywood would have nabbed any of June Capel, Clarissa Churchill, Pat Douglas, Veronica Fraser, Jane Kenyon-Slaney, Sylvia Muir, Sissie Lloyd Thomas, Elizabeth Scott or Gina Wernher.

Our lives were ruled by invitations, lists of girls and young men, trying to keep up with clean, white-kid gloves, including elbow-length ones for the evening that gave such style to the wearer, and shoes that suffered from being danced in all night. I longed for another evening dress. Mine were home-made by our retired housekeeper (£1 a time) but some of the girls had enviable clothes from Victor Stiebel and mothers who were dressed by Molyneux or Norman Hartnell. Hats came from Madame Rita in Berkeley Square. We wore silk stockings in London and lisle in the country and all the extras that seemed so essential then.

It was at the beginning of the 1938 season that the new US ambassador to the Court of St James arrived with much friendly publicity. Joseph P. Kennedy, his wife and nine children were warmly welcomed to London. Such a crowd of good-looking boys and girls had never been seen before among diplomats and they made an impact that was never forgotten.

The fourth of the nine was eighteen-year-old Kathleen, called Kick. Her initiation into the English season was to spend a weekend at Cliveden where the American Nancy Astor was the most famous hostess in this country. The Astors had four sons. The two youngest, Michael and Jakie, inherited their mother's brilliant talent to amuse and were the best company for any girl lucky enough to be invited to that Thames-side palace. Kick was understandably nervous when she arrived among the typical Cliveden mixture of young and old, politicians and religious leaders from all over the world, with the Astor boys poking fun at pompous guests as only they knew how. She emerged with flying colours, having charmed the lot of them.

Kick fell happily into this frenzied social activity and became the centre of attention. She was not strictly beautiful but differed from English girls in her infectious high spirits, lack of shyness, ability to play games, as well as talk politics with the older generation. Above all, her shining niceness came through. Because of her charm and lack of cattiness, none of us natives resented her, in spite of her success with the young men who were fascinated by the American phenomenon. She had the advantage of having two older brothers, Joe junior and Jack, who could take her around with her mother's consent.

The Kennedys lived in Princes Gate, round the corner from my father's house in Rutland Gate. There was much coming and going between the houses in company with Billy Hartington, Dawyck Haig, Andrew Cavendish, Hugh Fraser, David Ormsby Gore, William Douglas Home, Charlie Lansdowne and his brother Ned Fitzmaurice, the Astor boys, Charles Granby, Mark Howard, Robert and Dicky Cecil and various Woods and Stanleys – all undergraduates at Oxford or Cambridge.

Joe Kennedy junior was handsome and dashing but he preferred more sophisticated women to us eighteen-year-olds. Jack, who was just twenty-one, already had something about him that separated him from the crowd. He was very thin, the legacy of serious illnesses, but he put everything into the moment, which in 1938 was to enjoy himself. My mother, watching him at a dance and impressed by what she saw, said to Andrew, who never forgot it, 'I wouldn't be surprised if that young man became president of the United States.'

A year later came the war. The frivolities of living for pleasure ended with a bang, and we all went our separate ways. Kick and her family returned to the States, but she had made lifelong friends in London and was soon back wearing American Red Cross uniform. Billy Hartington had been one of her crowd of suitors for some time. He eventually won the prize against all comers and, after what seemed endless negotiations over her Catholic and his avowed Protestant faith, a compromise was reached about any children they might have. They were married in London on 6 May 1944.

The double tragedy that was to follow is well known. The Hartingtons spent only five weeks together before Billy's battalion was ordered to France. On 10 September he was killed by a sniper's bullet. After four years of widowhood, the twenty-eight-year-old Kick fell in love with Peter Fitzwilliam, another of those irresistibly attractive men who loved her. They were planning to marry and were on their way to the South of France in a small chartered plane when it crashed in a storm over the Alps and all on board were killed. So a life of such promise was extinguished. Kick is buried in the churchyard at Edensor, by Chatsworth Park. On her headstone is engraved, 'Joy she gave. Joy she has found.'

To all of us who had known and loved her it was impossible to believe that she was dead, just as it was impossible fifteen years later to believe that Jack had been assassinated. The sheer vitality of brother and sister made us think them immortal. Alas, they were not.

May 2006

PRESIDENT KENNEDY'S
INAUGURATION, 1961

After the marriage of Andrew's brother, Billy, to Kathleen (Kick) Kennedy, and their tragic deaths, Andrew, his two sisters and I were treated as part of the family by the Kennedys. This was the reason for our invitation to the inauguration of John Fitzgerald Kennedy as president of the United States of America in January 1961. Andrew was intrigued by the invitation and also realised what an honour it was to be asked. I did not want to go. There were engagements I was looking forward to at home, including the last shoot of the season. But it was so good of them to think of us that we accepted and set off for this unique celebration. The British ambassador, Sir Harold Caccia, and his wife put us up. These are the notes I made at the time.

The jumble of impressions of the last three days is so thick with oddness and general amazement it's very difficult to put them in any sort of order. The utter sweetness of our ambassador, Andrew hopping about being humble and saying that his job as parliamentary under-secretary makes him a very junior minister, the deliciousness of the brekker, the warmth of the embassy, the dread coolth of outdoors, the friendliness of the Kennedys and the extraordinary informality of the most solemn moments. My word, it is an odd country.

Thursday 19 January
The first day was mercifully quiet after the journey, which was very long (we came down at Shannon for some strange reason,

83

also the plane from New York was late so we arrived at the embassy at what was 4.30 a.m. for us, having left London at 2 p.m. the day before – fourteen and a half hours).

They raked in some embassy people for lunch, so that was easy. Then it started to snow and it snowed and snowed, and although Snow Plans A, B, C *and* D were put into operation, the capital city of the USA pretty well seized up, as they are not prepared for such an eventuality. Cars were abandoned in the middle of streets; engines chuck it very easily it seems and snow gets packed under the mudguards so that the wheels won't go round.

We were given tickets for the gala performance which was to raise money for the Democrats, who are $4 million in debt after the election (seats $1,000). So we buggered off to the place called the Armory, which is about twice the size of Olympia and the same idea. The embassy gave us a car while we were there, a very old-fashioned English thing called an Austin Princess. It took two and a half hours to get to the blooming Armory. It should have taken twenty minutes but the traffic was solid and so many cars broke down in the queue to get there. Our heater broke and I had only a fur cape, my word it was bitter. Andrew panicked all the way as the tickets said we had to be there at 8.30 and the President Elect was due at 9.00. At about 10.00 he said we'd better give it up and go home but luckily we couldn't as we were hemmed in on all sides by dread cars. The cold was extreme, about twenty degrees of frost, snowing hard and a bitter wind.

We finally loomed and by a miracle arrived at a very good time, viz. about ten minutes before the Kennedys. We needn't have worried as people were coming and going all the time, which we weren't to know. I thought it would be like a royal do in England but it was far from it.

We had marvellous seats, next to the Kennedys' box and between two very grand senators and their wives, who looked slightly down their noses at two complete strangers having such good places, till various Kennedys came and were fearfully nice, especially Bobby (who turns out to be attorney general with a staff of 35,000) who hugged us. Old Joe Kennedy, that well-known hater of England and the English, was very welcoming, and to crown all Jack came and said hello, to the astonishment of our senatorial neighbours.

The performance included all my favourites: Frank Sinatra, Jimmy Durante, Nat King Cole, Ethel Merman, Tony Curtis, Ella Fitzgerald, to mention a few, also Laurence Olivier and the chief American opera singer called Helen Traubel, who sang in a huge voice some ridiculous verses about the Kennedys' baby. It was WONDERFUL, especially at the finale when they had all done their turns and they ended up doing skits on popular songs with topical words. So unrehearsed were they that they had to read their lines and somehow it *was* so funny, just like Women's Institute theatricals at home, but when one looked again, there were all those famous faces. I adored all that.

We got home at 3 a.m. The heat in the house was fantastic. I opened all windows and slept with one blanket but it was still BOILING.

Friday 20 January
Next day was the actual inauguration. Left the embassy about 10 a.m. in order to be in our places at 11. Long queues of cars as we neared the Capitol. Anyone of note – ambassadors, senators, governors of States – had their name or country on the side of the car. We were next to some ratty-looking souls from Bulgaria in one traffic block, it made one think.

Eventually arrived at the Capitol. Horrid getting out as it was *so* cold with a cruel wind. The ambassadress had given me some long nylon stockings and knickers combined, also some rubber boots to put over my shoes. It was fearfully cold *with* these things – without them, heaven knows, I think I would have frozen to death. They gave Andrew a flask of whiskey but he still shivered throughout and put his scarf round his head (like the Queen).

We were told to wear top hats and smart things – both absolutely unnecessary as people were dressed for the Arctic. Some women had come in ridiculous flowered hats, which they soon covered up with scarves, rugs and anything to hand.

It was difficult to find our seats, no one knew where anything was, not even the few policemen who were about. When we eventually found our places they were very good for seeing – we were on street level, immediately in front of the Capitol where the ceremony was to take place, on a large balcony, high up but all plainly visible. Our seats were wooden strips, no backs, no floor and snow everywhere. No numbers or reserved places, one just sat where one liked on forms like at a school treat. Next to us were two Pakistanis with cameras. Just in front of me was old Mrs Roosevelt who had arrived an hour before we did and must have been terribly cold. The organisation seemed so vague I was afraid it would all be very late and we would be pillars of ice but in fact it started only a quarter of an hour after the appointed time.

The balcony of the Capitol was full of senators and congress-men sitting either side of the roofed pavilion from where Jack was to speak. The Capitol is faced with gleaming white marble and looked fine against the blue sky and snow, though the dome is painted just off-white, which slightly spoils the brilliant effect. Various members of the Kennedy family arrived. The girls – Eunice, Pat and Jean – were without hats, which seemed surprising for such a formal event. One could pick out the Eisenhowers, Trumans – Margaret and hubby – old Joe and Mrs Kennedy, but they were about the only people I knew by sight. Nixon and Mrs soon joined them.

Tension was mounting for Jack's arrival but it was badly arranged from a dramatic point of view – so different from things in England. No proper path was made for him through the crowd – people started shouting and suddenly there he was. Jackie looked very smart indeed in plain clothes of pale beige; the only woman who looked dressed at all.

There was a long pause after his arrival. People were cold and were stamping their feet. The star was there but nothing was happening. Eventually, the master of ceremonies announced some tune by the band and a famous gospel singer, Mahalia Jackson, whom I'd never heard of, sang 'The Star-Spangled Banner'. Then the swearing-in and four prayers – Roman Catholic cardinal, Jewish rabbi, Greek Orthodox priest and a Protestant – all much too long and not at all moving or impressive. Nobody paid the slightest attention and even the senators took photographs throughout, moving about to get in better positions. Some people in our row didn't stand up for the prayers. My Pakistani neighbour, at the third one, gave me a wink and said, 'Let's sit this one out', which I was going to do anyway as the rug fell in the snow every time we stood up.

Jack's speech was wonderful, the *words* were so good, almost biblical. Everyone was thankful to get up and move when it was over as we could only think of getting out of the cold and wind. We were told there was a bus reserved for the Kennedy family which we were to get on, but it seemed impossible to find. No one knew anything and there was no official-looking person to ask. After pushing and shoving and, in desperation, even stopping to ask a police car, we found it at last and the relief of getting into an overheated bus was wonderful.

In the bus we found Eunice and her husband (whose Christian name is Sargent, if you please, *fearfully* nice though). We were driven to a hotel for lunch with the family and close friends. Lots of grandchildren milling about, lots of delicious buffet food. Jack and Jackie, and Bobby and Ethel had lunch in the Capitol with the Cabinet, so weren't there. Back into the bus (which had a label on it 'Kennedy Family' like 'Chatsworth Tours') and through the guarded gates into the garden of the White House, whereupon all the people in the bus gave a loud cheer, led by Eunice, and shouted 'Here we are'.

As I got into the hall of the White House, a Marine stepped

forward, gave me his arm and armed me all the way through the house to the president's stand, from where we watched the parade. Andrew and I had seats several rows back. (All the seats were marked with people's names. The Marine asked me mine, I said, 'Devonshire', so he said, 'Mrs Devon*shyer*, you are heeere.') Next to us were Mr and Mrs Charles Wrightsman, who never turned up because they thought it too cold. The box had a roof and was enclosed at the sides with perspex but it was still extremely draughty and bitterly cold, even though there were army rugs on each seat.

The stands were gimcrack and the decorations practically nil, just a few small flags. Queer for such a rich country. The diplomats were next to us, sitting on raised forms, completely in the open. The Eastern ones looked so cold I felt terribly sorry for them as there was no escape and they couldn't leave till the parade was over.

The parade itself was an extraordinary mixture of army, navy and air force with girls' bands, majorettes in fantastic uniforms with long legs in pink tights, crinolined ladies on silver-paper floats, horses from the horsy states all looking a bit moth-eaten, army tanks, dread missiles (rhymes with 'epistles') on carriers, bands everywhere. One man marching by in an air-force contingent broke ranks, whipped out a camera, took a photograph of the president and joined in again. Imagine a Coldstream guardsman doing the same at the Trooping of the Colour.

The television cameras and a host of other photographers were immediately opposite the president's stand. The cameras were on him the whole afternoon. The informality was so queer – the president drinking coffee and eating a biscuit as the parade marched by. But he stood there for over three hours.

After about an hour and a half a message came, Would I go and sit beside him. It was the oddest feeling I've ever had, finding myself a sort of consort, standing by this man, talking to him during lapses in the parade. The telly people were stumped by the advent of a strange English lady; they knew the politicians and the film stars but not ordinary foreigners. We told Sir Harold Caccia when we got back and he said no English woman had ever done that before, so I *did* feel pleased.

Jack Kennedy has got an aura all right and he was obviously enjoying it all so much. After about three-quarters of an hour he said would we like to go with his father to the White House for tea, which I took to mean I'd been there long enough. The White House is very good inside, big rooms covered in silk, one dark red, one dark green, a huge creamish-coloured ballroom and a rather awful round room covered in a horrid blue Adam-design silk, which everyone seemed to like best. The diner is green, I'm sorry to say, painted solid gloomy green, pillars and all. Pictures of presidents all over the shop, all ghoulish.

We didn't see the president again as he was still at the parade when we left after tea. Got back to the embassy about 6.15 to be told dinner at 7.15, so I rushed to dress for the ball. Luckily I didn't take a tiara, which various people said I ought to have done, as no one wore one and I would have looked like a daft opera singer dressed up for Wagner. Mercifully only the Caccias for dinner. Afterwards we were taken by them to a party given by some cinema people. Lots of ambassadors and grandees there, a sort of after-dinner cocktail party. They don't mind the press like we do, and no wonder as they write in a very different way from ours, perfectly friendly and no sting in it.

Then back to the Armory for the Inaugural Ball. This time no traffic jam and we arrived without difficulty. All the seating at floor level had been removed and a vast dancing floor put in its place. Shown to the president's box again, where we sat until someone said there was drink and a telly in a room at the back. So we made off there and saw Mrs David Bruce, a friend of Nancy [Mitford]'s, rather beautiful and probably coming to London with her husband as ambassador. Without any warning, the president suddenly walked into the room and was taken off to a television interview next door. Meanwhile we watched his inaugural speech again on the telly.

Back to the presidential box to watch the dancing, which didn't happen because everyone stood looking up at the box, waiting for Jack to appear. When he did he got terrific applause. He didn't go down to the dance floor but talked to various people along his row. Wherever he goes he is like a queen bee, surrounded by photographers, detectives, nexts of kin and worshippers. By this time, we were sitting in the topmost tier just below the roof. As Jack came back along the first row, fenced in as usual by humans, he saw us, broke away and climbed over seven rows of seats to say goodbye, to the utter astonishment of the people sitting either side of us. A photographer who had got, as he thought, a very bad place and who had been grumbling, was now able to take the closest close-up of all.

I told Jack about Unity [Mitford]'s letter of twenty-one years ago saying how he was going to have a terrific future. I also asked him if he knew Harold Macmillan and he said he was going to see him soon. We said how we were loving everything that had been arranged for us, to which he replied that we'd stuck it well. He and Jackie then left. We waited till some of the crush had dispersed and thought we'd leave too. Andrew went out into the bitter night to look for the chauffeur – no sign of him. Eventually he was found, the car had broken and there we were with no hope of getting home. After an hour and a half the chauffeur suggested we take Labour leader Mr Gaitskell's car and send it back for him. By a miracle we saw Gaitskell among the 10,000 people there and thankfully squashed into his car, me sitting on a drunken lady who answered 'balls' to everything I said.

Saturday 21 January
We went to the Senate the next day, taken by a new senator's wife who had lunched at the embassy. Hideous place; they each have a desk and chair, like in school. Andrew went into the Chamber

(they have a reciprocal agreement with members of certain foreign governments) and two senators immediately launched into speeches of welcome. I was sweating in case he would make one back but he only bowed. Good old Andrew.

The upshot of the whole outing is two new bodies to worship – Sir Harold Caccia and Jack Kennedy. I've written him a letter beginning 'My Dear Jack'. I do hope I won't have my head cut off for impertinence. One of the comical things was that Andrew had some secrets from Harold Macmillan to tell the ambassador and nothing was said until we all went to bed on the last night, when I heard them talking in the passage outside my room for hours. I can see that's the way things are done in high life, very odd.

PRESIDENT KENNEDY'S FUNERAL, 1963

President Kennedy was murdered in Texas on 22 November 1963 and his funeral was held in Washington three days later. Andrew and I were offered places in the plane chartered for HRH Prince Philip, who was representing the Queen, to attend the funeral. Also on board were the Prime Minister, Sir Alec Douglas-Home, and Lady Home; the Leader of the Opposition, Harold Wilson; the PM's private secretaries, Sir Philip de Zulueta and Sir Timothy Bligh; Prince Philip's valet and three girl secretaries, two of whom had stayed with us at Bolton Abbey and Chatsworth when working for Harold Macmillan. After the funeral, I made the following notes.

Sunday 24 November

Left Chatsworth with Andrew at 12.40 to drive to London airport. Found Mr Wilson in the VIP lounge. Talked to Marie-Louise de Zulueta, who had come to see her husband off. The PM and his wife arrived soon afterwards. Prince Philip arrived exactly on time. We got into the plane at 4.50 and took off at 5.10. There were headwinds of 140 mph that slowed us up and the flight took nine hours.

It was a huge Boeing 707. There were 150 empty seats behind us – something I have never seen before. Prince Philip called us up to his seats in front and asked Mr Wilson to join him for dinner. I sat next to Wilson with the Prince opposite, and Andrew sat with the Douglas-Homes on the other side of the aisle.

My lot started talking about aeroplanes (a safe subject, I suppose) in such an incredible, almost technical, way that it was quite impossible to listen to them and I found my mind wandering. Wilson had such dirty fingernails it put me off dinner. I wished I was with Andrew and the Homes but kept thinking how extremely odd the company and that I ought to be interested, but it was impossible to be so. Wilson has a level, grating voice and podgy face with a too small nose. After dinner tried to sleep a bit.

When below was all lights on the east coast of America, the sad reason for the journey hit me again and I dreaded arriving. We were met by a 'mobile lounge', a vast bus-like thing with room for many more people than we were. Our ambassador, David Ormsby Gore, and his wife, Sissie, looking red-eyed and worn out, the secretary of state, Dean Rusk, whose face was puffed up, and some others welcomed us on the tarmac and joined us on the bus.

At the terminal were the Commonwealth ambassadors, including nice George Laking from New Zealand with whom I'd had tea on my last visit. Television cameras and lights, then a procession of about six cars with police sirens at front and rear. Twenty-two miles into Washington and no stopping at red lights. It was a strange feeling arriving at the embassy. We had a drink and short talk in the drawing room before, thankfully, going to bed.

David said that Bobby Kennedy was taking the brunt; not only was he bitterly sad himself and having to deal with arrangements that were chaotic because of everything being at such short notice, but also he was the one person who could comfort Jackie. He said that General de Gaulle was the only head of state who had demanded to see Jackie, so she said she would see them all. Jack's belongings have already been removed from his office and bedroom and the White House has taken on a deserted look.

Sissie said that Mass at the White House for friends and the

Catholics who worked there was the most tragic thing she ever saw – everyone crumpled with grief.

Monday 25 November
Prince Philip, the prime minister and David left for St Matthew's Cathedral before we did, as they were to walk in the procession from the White House. Andrew and I, Sissie, and Prince Philip's ADC left at about 11 a.m. Brilliant sunshine, frosty day with bright blue sky. We arrived at the Cathedral without a hitch. It is not very big and has only about 2,000 seats. We were all seated separately as the pews reserved for friends were already full. I was on an aisle, having arrived late, and the people already in the pew moved up for me. Prince Philip seemed very far towards the back of the church. Apparently he had no seat and the Douglas-Homes had moved to make room for him.

When I could bring myself to look round, I saw Jayne Wrightsman and behind her Fifi Fell, as beautiful as ever. There was no music for a long time. I never saw so many sad faces and when Jack's great friends came in – Bill Walton, Chuck Spalding, Evelyn Lincoln, Charles Bartlett, Arthur Schlesinger, MacGeorge Bundy – it was too much. Then the family arrived with Jack's two little children. Rose Kennedy looking small and hunched and Bobby too. Eunice, Jean and Pat with no veils but wearing black-lace mantillas, their faces set and staring and so so sad.

The coffin was carried by eight soldiers. It was impossible to believe that the vital, fascinating and clever person was shut up in that box. Quite impossible.

The service, luckily, was incomprehensible and the cardinal faced the altar most of the time. No agonising hymns, so it seemed far away and impersonal. There was Communion in the middle and quite a lot of people besides the family went up to the altar. On our way into the church, the Scotch pipers had played very fidgety music, as had the military band. We heard afterwards that it was because they do not do a slow march here, so it does not sound nearly as solemn as in England.

On the way out of the church, the overseas visitors stopped several times and for a full minute General de Gaulle stood next to me. He has the strangest appearance I ever saw – very tall, yet collapsed somehow and a long ugly nose. Haile Selassie looked fine – small and beautiful. The rest looked as they do in their photographs.

Our car arrived wonderfully quickly and we followed the procession to the cemetery. When it began to go at a slow pace, the secret service men – who were guarding Prince Philip, Alec Douglas-Home, De Gaulle and the Canadian prime minister, Lester Pearson – all got out and walked three-a-side of each car. There were crowds all the way for the three miles to the cemetery, which is on the side of a hill and beautiful. We arrived just as the last part of the service had begun. Aeroplanes flew overhead, including the president's plane that we'd seen at Lincolnshire airport in June when Jack came to Chatsworth. Prince Philip was jostled to the back again, behind a lot of soldiers, so he was not among the foreign visitors when they came away from the grave. The Russians were completely enclosed by secret service people. I saw Colonel Glenn and that ghastly Queen of Greece with her dangling earrings, and many famous faces mixed up with police and hangers-on, who were all ambling about in the bright sun waiting for cars. Jackie looked tragic, with tears glistening on her veil, and Rose so very pathetic. The Kennedys are so good when things are going well but they are not equipped for tragedy.

We drove back to the embassy through thinning crowds. There was a great sense of sorrow and emptiness everywhere. We drank a lot of tea. I was very tired, as were all – we had left at 11.00 and got back about 4.00. Andrew went up to change and pack. Prince Philip went to Lyndon Johnson's reception at the White House. We watched it on television and, as usual, De Gaulle hogged the limelight. He arrived late so there was much speculation as to where he was and, when he did arrive, all was focused on him. The TV commentator was not too nice about Prince Philip or Sir Alec. Andrew and the Prince left for New York in an air-force jet and then on to London on a scheduled flight, Mr Wilson in tow.

The Canadians came for dinner – Ambassador Charles Ritchie with his talkative wife, Lester Pearson and his wife and their foreign secretary, Paul Martin, who had to go to the lav in the middle of dinner. David and Sissie looked slightly better, I thought. The very fact of having to have people in the house is probably a good thing; having to go on with ordinary life, though the outlook here is very bleak for them. They came and talked for ages in my room. Very, very sad, but we talked about other things. I wonder so much what David will do. No doubt he will have to stick out another year as ambassador here, which must be an awful prospect. It will be very difficult working with the new administration – no intimacy, no shared memories and no jokes.

Tuesday 26 November
The prime minister went to see Lyndon Johnson and came back saying he was friendly, tried to make a good impression and said that he would carry out Jack's foreign policy, etc. David said the White House was completely changed. Jackie had wanted to move by today but has put it off till Friday.

I went over to Eunice and found her perfectly extraordinary, laughing almost as if the thing had never happened, yet talking about everything in the past tense. We walked round her house about twelve times. How awful to live in a place where you can't go for a proper walk. Horses and dogs everywhere and one little boy aged about three. Bill Walton came for lunch, so nice, and both were wonderfully cheerful and talking about a memorial for Jack and what it should be. They suggested a long street from the White House to the Capitol, paved in different colours and with graded heights so people could see processions etc.

It seems Jackie has been extraordinary, planning everything with Bobby to do with the funeral. She was even laughing about going to see Johnson as the widder woman with lowered eyes and asking him to carry on various things Jack had been interested in. She is going to live in Georgetown it seems.

I left with Bill, having telephoned Bobby who said I could go and see him. His house is near the road and had a few sloppy policemen outside it. A man opened the door in his shirtsleeves. Jack's special assistant, Kenny O'Donnell, was there. Bobby and Ethel have built on a big drawing room, a lovely room, where there was a cot for the new baby. Ethel came in looking about seventeen – it's impossible to believe she has eight children. She's so terribly nice and good. I love her. Then Bobby arrived in a dressing gown which did not reach his knees and all hairy like an animal from top to bottom, but a v. lovable face and stout legs. I did not stay long. The house was in turmoil, telephones going everywhere.

Back to the embassy. Much chatting with Elizabeth Home, who is cast in the same mould as Dorothy Macmillan – a large reassuring body and great niceness pervading all. Johnny Walker, director of the Washington National Gallery, and his Scottish wife came for drinks. Then the Russian ambassador, Anastas Mikoyan, suddenly turned up with interpreters. An odd roomful.

For dinner came Joe and Susan Mary Alsop, Ted Sorensen – Jack's special counsellor – and his girlfriend and Bill Walton. Sorensen scarcely spoke all evening. Sissie says he is one of the worst affected of all. I sat next to the prime minister. He says his brother, William Douglas-Home, has written a play about a peer who gives up his title to become PM. What a surprise. Had a talk with Joe Alsop after dinner about Mollie Salisbury and Pamela Egremont and their different roles in life. Everyone left quite early and we went to bed because of the early start. Somehow the atmosphere has lifted a bit but I would not stay here for *anything* and long to get out of it.

Called at 6.45. Quick breakfast downstairs with everyone. Sissie and David came to the airport in an overheated mobile lounge and suddenly the atmosphere was like that at our arrival. Did not say much. Felt David so overwhelmed again with pent-up emotion. He kissed me goodbye – something he has never done before. I feel a strong bond with him. He loved Jack so much and saw the funniness better than anyone.

I do not know what I remember most about these strange two days, which is all it was though it seemed like three months. Perhaps it was three-year-old John Kennedy leaving the church, touching the flag on the coffin and being led away by some huge man, followed by a sobbing nanny; or General de Gaulle standing just by me as he waited for the heads of state to leave the church; or Prince Philip's stern blue look as he stood in the same place while tears poured down my face; or Dean Rusk all crumpled when he came to meet our PM; or Chuck Spalding and Bill Walton as they arrived at church; or Fifi Fell's beautiful face in a trance at the end; or David and Sissie, blotchy and thin – I came away feeling so terribly sorry for them that words were impossible. The light has gone out for so many people and for David and Sissie it has been a hammer blow.

Besides the secretaries, there were only the Douglas-Homes, Liberal leader Jo Grimond and me in the PM's vast chartered plane on the way home. Went across the aisle to talk to Mr Grimond, who is charming and woolly and hopeless but sees the point, very quick. The four of us had lunch together. It was dark outside because of the time change. Any strain there may have been soon wore off. We had a friendly talk as politicians do with people of opposing convictions, yet there sat the man, Grimond, who is probably going to do-in any chance Home has of getting back at the next election. Sir Alec's sweet string vest showed through his shirt. He has a strange, saintly streak, so quiet and calm and good. When Elizabeth Home and Jo Grimond were talking, the PM said he had wanted to make David OG foreign secretary but Rab Butler had said he wouldn't serve unless he was given the job. Home evidently has a tremendous regard for David. His patience is extraordinary.

About half an hour before we were due into London, a message came to say there was fog and that we would have to land at Prestwick or Manchester. I said do let's go to Manchester and all come to Chatsworth for the night. They politely said they must get back to London whatever happened. In the end we made for Manchester. I repeated my invitation and sent messages for cars to meet us.

We arrived at Chatsworth at about 11 p.m., after what seemed an endless journey. House floodlit. Dennis, Bryson and Henry standing at the door. It all looked warm and welcoming. The only sad thing was no flowers in the rooms. Jo Grimond, Harold Evans – the PM's public relations adviser – Timothy Bligh and Philip de Zulueta all turned up. Sir Alec said if he crept into bed and lay very still we would not have to change the sheets for Princess Margaret who was coming the next day.

I so wished they could have stayed the weekend but they were called at 6.30 and to catch the 7.24 train. They arrived and left in the dark.

'THE TREASURE HOUSES OF BRITAIN'
EXHIBITION IN WASHINGTON

On 31 October 1985, I was lucky enough to go to the National Gallery of Art in Washington for the private opening of 'The Treasure Houses of Britain: 500 Years of Private Patronage and Art Collecting'. It was the culmination of nearly five years of planning for the organisers. The director of the gallery, J. Carter Brown, is a young man of great energy and knowledge, both directed at the success of his gallery. He has a love of England and English things and has long been fascinated by what he has seen in houses here.

In summer 1981, Carter Brown and his wife stayed at Chatsworth for a weekend and later he told me that the idea for the exhibition came to him then. He wrote to Andrew soon afterwards to enlist his support and no doubt also wrote to many other owners, most of whom were willing to lend. One of the difficulties was the timing. Nearly all the houses are open for six or seven months of the year and could not spare their best things during that time, so Carter Brown was limited to the winter months for his show.

A sponsor was soon found in the Ford Motor Company. The two governments provided the horrendous sum for insurance and the plan was under way. The masterstroke of the organisers was the appointment of Gervase Jackson-Stops, the National Trust's architectural adviser, as chooser and collector of the works of art. He came to Chatsworth many times in search of what he called 'D.O.'s', Desirable Objects, and each time he added something he said he MUST have. No doubt he did the same at Burghley House, Castle Howard, Woburn Abbey and the rest. Such is his charm, with an appalling stammer that he does not give in to, and his unrivalled knowledge and memory of what is where, Andrew found it impossible to refuse him anything. He would be the best burglar ever. He and Carter Brown commuted between Washington and England for months, choosing and persuading the owners till they got (very nearly) everything they wanted.

When they had completed the list of D.O.'s from Chatsworth, Andrew got a letter saying Thank you very much, it is very kind of you to lend so much but they are all dirty and lots are broken, so will you please have them cleaned and mended before they go? No, I will not, answered Andrew. You can either have them as they are or you can't have them at all. I believe other owners answered in the same sort of way, so poor old Gervase was in a bit of a fix. I don't know how he and Carter managed it but in the event the Getty Foundation paid for cleaning and restoration. The glowing condition of the D.O.'s will make the pairs to those returning look a bit glum.

You have no idea (but I'm sure you have) of the time it takes to pack and send such an extraordinary collection of objects, varying in size, make and shape, from Canova's *Three Graces* from Woburn Abbey to a Fabergé snuff box from Luton Hoo, not to mention Lady Lambton's tiara and the colossal marble foot from the Chapel Passage at Chatsworth. The great packing began in July 1985 and the last things left Chatsworth in early October. Each had its own box or packing case, made to measure and lined with the sort of thing I wish my mattress was made of, so they reclined in luxury and safety while crossing the Atlantic until unpacked with tender care by the white-gloved lads at the National Gallery. We were given photographs of what was taken and these were put up where the missing objects belong, with a notice saying 'This Work of Art . . .' to explain their absence.

Meanwhile the National Gallery nearly lost its director. When Carter Brown was driving from Chatsworth to Castle Howard in the summer of 1984, he went the wrong way down a dual carriageway of the A1 and had a head-on crash with a lorry. He was badly hurt and spent weeks in hospital in York. Fortunately, he made a good recovery but it left him with a lot of pain from broken bones.

I happened to be in Washington six months before the exhibition opened. At the time, Gervase and the Gallery's brilliant designers were working from models of the proposed rooms, with all the objects cut out to scale. The part of the Gallery set aside for the exhibition was then just high white walls without a hint of the transformation that was to take place during the summer.

As time drew near for the private view, the organisers set themselves another fearful task – as though they hadn't already done enough. They planned a dinner at the National Gallery for the lenders and, more complicated still, they arranged for us all to be entertained at dinner the following night in private houses in Washington. Now Washington hostesses are famous, as we who are old enough to remember the musical *Call Me Madam* will know. I would not have wanted to be the person to decide who dined with whom and I believe the lobbying for bagging the more so-called glamorous of the English guests was interesting.

A tour of Virginia houses was also arranged, which lasted several days, and this was taken up by many of the lenders and was greatly appreciated and enjoyed by all who took part. One thing which delighted me was that it never stopped raining all the time we were there. I shall never feel guilty again when our American guests find they have hit a wet spell in this country.

To return to the exhibition, I went round at leisure four times. I should have liked to see it forty more. It is the best exhibition

I have ever seen, really faultless. It isn't often you can say that about anything. Inside that ultra-modern building, the designers recreated rooms from Tudor times till now, embellished with things familiar and unfamiliar. They chose not only the great works of art, known by all interested in such things, but curiosities and very private possessions – a number of which had been most generously lent by people whose houses are not open to the public. I say that, and underline it, because it is obviously good for a house like Chatsworth to be represented, but for someone like Lord Halifax, for instance, to lend his superb Titian, *Portrait of a Young Man*, is very public-spirited indeed. I remember seeing it in his human-sized drawing room in Yorkshire. It gives you the shock of recognition of genius. Nothing can compare with the way the Young Man seemed to be not just on canvas but in the room and ready to talk with the rest of the company. Such pictures on exhibition always start a spate of enquiries from people wanting a special visit to a private house, besides which there is security to be considered.

There is no charge to go to the exhibition but visitors pass through a turnstile so numbers are known. You enter a huge modern building with one or two shockingly ugly mobiles floating overhead. Then the first room takes you straight into an atmosphere of Hatfield House or Haddon Hall or Penshurst Place. The jewel-like beauty of the Elizabethan portraits and the extraordinary *Lumley Horseman* (carved in oak and painted in oils, with stirrups, bit and axe made of iron – the earliest known equestrian statue, from Lumley Castle, Durham) silence the crowds who seem to have wandered into church.

The next room is redolent of Hardwick Hall or Parham Park – a Long Gallery faithfully reproduced. The windows are leaded; the ever so slightly tinted glass was made in Germany. There is matting on the floor, admittedly not rush but the nearest thing to it, and the portraits of royal people, explorers and other worthies in the extravagant clothes of the time warrant going all the way to Washington to see. Of all the rooms in the exhibition perhaps this Long Gallery reminds you most of the real thing.

From here you pass into a sort of giant silver-cupboard dominated by a glass-fronted wall of shelves, laden with incredible objects, from the jewelled Beaufort garter badges from Badminton to the vast Burghley wine cooler – a silver bath of fearsome proportions which was one of the extravagances the press fastened on in their reviews.

Every now and again I came across something familiar in these most unfamiliar surroundings and I began consciously to look for Chatsworth things while other lenders looked for theirs. It reminded me of before the war when it was the fashion at smart weddings to display the presents. On one occasion my mother had been much amused by an old couple going round tables covered in grand things saying, 'Where's our blotter?' Listening to the English voices was just like that, only it was, 'Where's our Rembrandt?'

When we reached the early to mid-eighteenth century, I felt more and more at home as Lord Burlington's loved possessions seemed almost to take over with the Grand Tour and what the guidebook refers to as 'Souvenirs from Italy'. Some souvenirs these! There is a room devoted to Lord Burlington and the Palladian Revolution, which has several pictures of Chiswick Villa with furniture and other designs by William Kent, Burlington's distinguished friend. Most of these are now at Chatsworth.

You progress to an Adam room. Not my favourite period with its small, finicky and ladylike designs, but I know I am in a minority and I have to admire the skill of its execution. Here one is impressed once more by the meticulous attention to detail of the designers. As in all the rooms, the cornices and other architectural details are faithfully reproduced. Some of the furniture is on plinths a few inches high, which gives them importance and ensures that they are not kicked by passing feet.

But the cleverness is that the plinths are made of polished boards of the same wood that was used for floors at the time when the furniture was made – oak in the earlier rooms, wide boards and other woods as we progress through the centuries. This little touch gives authenticity to the piece; it rings true. I don't think I noticed it the first time round but then it impressed me as much as the specially made silk on the walls, woven in Suffolk. The compilers of the catalogue are too modest to describe all that they did and there are no photographs of their 'rooms', but I hope somewhere all their huge efforts are documented. It would serve as a pattern for anyone trying to do something similar in the future.

All that is missing in this perfection is evidence of the *désordre britannique*, the hallmark of the English country house. A couple of toys (one broken), a sofa covered in newspapers, stray novels, an old dog flopped down by the fireplace and the smell of wet macs would have nailed any of the rooms as having been well and truly lived in by the same family in the same way for generations.

One of the two things in the show that attracted the most attention (along with the Burghley silver wine-cooler) is the bed from Calke Abbey. The bed is English with Chinese hangings – embroidery of coloured silks and gold thread, close-covered on an oak and pine framework. It has been illustrated in colour in *Country Life* and is striking because of its intricacy of detail and brilliant colours. (Some of the trimmings look as if they ought to be on a ball dress rather than a piece of furniture.) It's the very opposite of today's fashion for pastel colours and is very refreshing indeed. It was found in packing cases at Calke, having arrived probably in 1734, and was never set up – which accounts for its immaculate state of preservation.

I happened to be in the room with the bed while Henry Harpur Crewe of Calke was being interviewed by an American television company. It was as good as a play. His questioners were earnest and polite, so unlike their English counterparts who are neither. 'Is it true that this bed arrived in your house two hundred and fifty years ago and was *never unpacked*?' 'Yes, absolutely true.' Pause. 'Why was that?' 'Well, I suppose they had other things to do. Oh no, they didn't *unpack* it.' As though it was perfectly ordinary, which of course it was at Calke. I couldn't resist saying, 'Henry, do get into that bed.' And then the television people knew they were among a lot of loonies.

And so you progress to the Rotunda, designed to show sculptures, through the Regency furniture and on to Victorian pictures where there are Landseers, including the dogs' *Trial by Jury* from Chatsworth, and a marvellous giant Edward Lear of a Corsican forest from Beaufront Castle. There is some amazing furniture from Osborne House, made from antlers and even stags' neatly divided slots (hooves), produced in Germany and belonging to the Queen.

Then on through Edwardian portraits by John Singer Sargent, John Lavery and Alfred Munnings. In Munnings' portrait *The Princess Royal on Portumna* (1930), the princess is painted on the grey horse given her as a wedding present by 'The Hunting Women of Ireland'. The artist and sitter had three consecutive sittings during the Craven meetings at Newmarket. Munnings described it as his 'best equestrian portrait', adding, 'The conditions under which I worked, including the weather, were the best I have ever known.'

In *Sybil Cholmondeley, Countess of Rocksavage* (1922), a late work by Sargent, the sitter wears a copy of a sixteenth-century court dress specially commissioned from Worth, which cost over £200. Artist and sitter had a 'month of sittings in the fog', after which Sargent announced, 'Sybil is *lovely*. Some days she is positively green', a compliment apparently.

There is a brightly-lit showcase with four tiaras and a library, which by its nature is almost impossible to reproduce satisfactorily, but the designers have made a good stab at it with some open books in showcases. The first day the exhibition was open to the public, I heard an English reporter ask a group of women what they liked best. Without hesitation they all said the tiaras. There is no accounting for taste. The doll's house from Nostell Priory attracts a great deal of attention; it is a wonder of its kind. I think the selectors began to lose heart after this and the present day tails off sadly, saved by some nostalgic photographs of house parties at Cliveden and elsewhere.

Not surprisingly, the exhibition had rave reviews from the press, with a few predictable exceptions. To give nothing but praise is more than journalists can bear and some papers had to be different. My son went on to Kentucky, to the centre of the American racing industry, and there an Irish-American paper had some rough stuff to say about the wicked English aristocrats grinding the faces of the poor to enable them to show off to one another by their extravagant purchases of works of art. The *New York Review of Books* gave a depressingly negative account, mostly directed at the owners because even that paper had to admit the quality of the exhibits. *American House & Garden* was scathing about the lenders in a tiresome, gossipy kind of way, but on the whole the reviewers gave it its due. Several have harped on the value of the exhibits and have hinted that because they have been chosen to go to Washington, their value has increased by 20 per cent (how they arrived at that figure I don't know) and that some owners will be inclined to sell, having had this unrivalled opportunity for inspection by American antique dealers and collectors. Time will show if these journalists are right.

As well as being generously entertained in private houses, as only Americans know how, we were also given tea at the White House by Mrs Reagan. This outing had its comic side. Among the heaps of paper with itinerary and invitations was an instruction that some other form of identification, as well as the invitation, must be produced for entry into the White House. Few of us had read or even noticed this, so we queued up at a lodge in the pouring rain while bemused guards had to decide if the motley crowd really were the Duke and Duchess of This-and-That or assassins. No one minded queuing or the rain – all are very used to both – but it was very funny indeed to see this rather bedraggled crowd of English grandees. One or two did look unlikely customers, chiefly Lord Neidpath who is always oddly dressed. For Mrs Reagan's tea he wore a dirty white suit with a broad black stripe, a high wing-collar and gym shoes, and he hadn't shaved for three days. However, he must have satisfied the police because I saw him at the sandwiches later on.

When we got to about tenth in the queue to meet Mrs Reagan, we were stopped by a policewoman who showed us how to shake hands – something that has never happened to me before, but now I know just how to do it. We all managed and the First Lady stood patiently as we filed by. Then we could wander about the rooms as we liked. They are most beautifully kept; everything in spanking condition and just as it should be, flowers, carpets and curtains all gleaming.

The dinner at the National Gallery was an eye-opener. In my long and spoilt life I have seen many wonderful entertainments but this had an originality which made it memorable. About four hundred people, I believe, all dressed in their best, which once in a while is a pleasure to see, were seated at round tables for eight. The tablecloths were made of flowery cotton – a nod to English chintz. Then something clever, which I have never seen before: on the tables, instead of the usual little bouquet of flowers of just the right height so you can see the people opposite, there were tall, narrow vases on plinths with a huge high arrangement – perfect for the immensely high space we were in. You couldn't call it a room, it was a sort of first-floor hall which goes to the roof.

The waiters in Washington are said to be out-of-work actors. I don't know whether this is so but they certainly act being waiters very well. They are handsome, smiling young men, apparently enjoying themselves as much as the guests and it is extraordinary how this atmosphere pervaded the whole place – a gala if ever there was one. I sat next to one Mr Schultz, who I suddenly realised was the foreign secretary, and on the other side Mr Petersen, the managing director of the Ford Motor Company.

The memory of all this excitement will remain with me. In tangible form there is the catalogue. 'It weighs as much as a salmon and is as difficult to hold,' someone said. True. It is also a work of scholarship, of utter fascination – history distilled through works of art. I cannot recommend it too strongly as a book to turn to for minutes or hours; every item is illustrated and it is beautifully written. Expensive, I know, but worth every penny.

March 1986

In 1995, dear good Gervase Jackson-Stops died. The unforgettable experience of this exhibition was due to him, more than anyone. I hope he realises, when he looks down on us who remain, how we all revelled in his creation.

MARBLE MANIA

'I have made several journeys into Italy, and at Rome the love of marble possesses most people like a new sense.' So wrote the 6th Duke of Devonshire, the 'Bachelor Duke', in his *Handbook of Chatsworth and Hardwick* of 1844.

On his first visit to Rome in 1819 he was indeed possessed. He soon translated his new passion into reality, and marbles, both ancient and modern, arrived at Chatsworth by the dozen. His first purchase, for £2,000, was of two alabastro cotognino columns which he described as 'the most beautiful in the world'. The now familiar story of an embargo on the export of antiquities put a stop to the transaction (Pope Pius VII claimed them for his new gallery at the Vatican) but the experience only increased the Bachelor Duke's desire for these wonders.

As always with the duke, friendship with an artist fuelled his wish to own some of the artist's work, and he held the charming Antonio Canova in high regard. He was introduced to the sculptor by his stepmother, Elizabeth Duchess of Devonshire (Bess Foster of the famous *ménage à trois* was his father's mistress and also the beloved friend of his mother, Georgiana). The widowed Bess lived in Rome where she organised and paid for what is now called a 'dig', which revealed the surrounding road and pavement in the Roman Forum as well as many fragments of antiquity.

The duke was often to be found in Canova's studio and before long he had acquired the seated figure of Napoleon's mother,

Madame Mère – 'The old lady herself used to receive me at Rome, and rather complained of my possessing her statue, though my belief is that it was sold for her advantage'; a bust of Madame Mère; a bust of Petrarch's Laura – 'entirely formed by his own chisel'; *Hebe*, bought from Lord Cawdor – '*Hebe* came on springs by post from Wales'; and a colossal head of Napoleon – 'Canova kept the large bust of Napoleon in his bed-room till his dying day. He finished it from the study of the colossal statue, now in the possession of the Duke of Wellington.'

The duke's favourite statue, *Endymion*, was commissioned by him from Canova. He was on tenterhooks when its arrival in this country was imminent, and his sister said it was no good talking to him, he could not concentrate and was beside himself with anticipation and worry. 'What anxiety for its voyage to England! A cast of it, sent from Leghorn to Havre, was lost at sea: it was to have been copied in bronze at Paris.' Often the long and hazardous sea voyage was too much for the safety of the precious cargo. Thorvaldsen's *Venus* arrived broken in three places – 'A bracelet, hiding the fracture of the arm, is one that the Princess Pauline procured when she went into mourning on the death of Napoleon, and she gave it me for this object.'

After Canova's death, which affected him greatly, the duke concentrated on other sculptors working in Rome, many of them pupils of Canova; he bought works on their merit but also perhaps to reflect his friendship with the master. Thomas Campbell took fourteen years to complete the seated figure of Princess Pauline Borghese – 'She was no longer young, but retained her beauty and charm . . . Campbell used to bring his modelling clay to a pavilion in her garden. The little luncheons on those occasions were delightful; for the Princess Borghese, when compelled not to talk about dress, was extremely entertaining and full of the histories of her time.'

At Chatsworth the duke's love of stone begins to show in the long wing that he added to the house in the 1820s. It was built by Wyatville and includes the Sculpture Gallery, designed to display his new passion. There is marble in every shape, colour and form: pillars, vases, plinths, urns, tazzas, table-tops, heads, bodies and legs of men, women and children, mythological wings supporting mythological horses, dogs, babies and snakes, in every pattern of salami, brawn, liver sausage, galantine, ballantine, pâté, ham mousse, veined Stilton cheese, Christmas pudding and mincemeat known to the buyer for a delicatessen.

In the crowd of gods and goddesses, emperors and vestals, you will find works by Kessel, Gibson, Tenerani, Thorvaldsen, Schadow, Albacini, Trentanove, Bartolini, Westmacott, Rinaldi, Campbell, Finelli, Tadolini – and a greyhound bitch and her puppies by Joseph Gott, 'the Landseer of marble'. But Canova remained the favourite. His tools are preserved behind a glass panel and are 'certainly the last he employed'.

So much for the Bachelor Duke's modern sculpture, which is such a feature at Chatsworth, admired again today as it was when first acquired. He was also an ardent collector of antiquities. At Smyrna in 1838, his catholic taste made him buy the Greek bronze head of Apollo, *c.* 470 BC, Chatsworth's most important antique sculpture. It is now in the British Museum, having been taken for death duties in the 1950s. Wisely, he kept ancient and modern apart. Under a draughty stone arch at the entrance to the garden, he arranged the bits and pieces of architectural and other fragments collected on his journeys. When we cleared an impenetrable mass of rhododendrons in the garden in the 1980s we found a Greek altar from the island of Milos – mentioned by the duke in his *Handbook* and hidden for a hundred years. Each piece held a particular memory for him of a place or person and he wrote their detailed descriptions in his *Handbook*. Many came from Canova's own collection, including a group noted by the duke as being 'rich, busy and pleasing' – words which conjure up the writer himself.

The most impressive and powerful of all are the two Egyptian figures of Sekhmet, goddess of war and strife, half-woman half-lion, hewn from dark granite, 'sent home by a famous traveller and purchased by me in the New Road'. These massive creatures are from the Temple of Mut at Karnak and date from *c.* 1360 BC. I can't make up my mind whether their powerful presence is malign or benign, but they certainly dominate the Chapel Passage.

Taste in works of art is notoriously susceptible to fashion and none more so than the neoclassical pieces in the Sculpture Gallery. Andrew's Granny, who reigned at Chatsworth from 1908 to 1938, detested them and tried to lose them by scattering pieces around the house and even in the garden. She considered them to be so much bulky trash. A nadir was reached in the 1950s when an inventory valued the whole collection, including six works by Canova, at under £1,000. The sculptures have not changed – taste has.

October 2001

BRUCE, MARIO, STELLA AND ME

In early summer 1995, the photographer Bruce Weber was working on Long Island with our granddaughter Stella Tennant, who is a model. Bruce was planning to come to England and asked Stella if she knew of a house, perhaps in the country, which would make a good background for pictures of her in the next season's clothes. So Stella telephoned to ask if they could come to Chatsworth. Bruce liked the idea of taking family pictures in a family house, so the plan was made.

The 'shoot', when Stella arrived with Bruce and his eleven assistants, was of a very different kind to when King Edward VII and Queen Alexandra came to shoot at the beginning of the last century. Pheasants were the target then and photographers were kept at bay.

The nursery was used as headquarters and in no time big trunks of clothes from some of the most famous fashion houses in Europe and America were unpacked and their contents hung on the portable rails usually kept near the entrance hall for people to hang coats when they arrive for charitable events. Three tables were covered in pairs of shoes of all colours of the rainbow, with the highest heels I ever saw. Bruce's team wasted no time in getting to work and Stella was soon sitting in a chair being made up.

Chatsworth has been much photographed and it is difficult for someone who has never been before to find a new site, but Bruce saw at once where he was to work and chose original places for

Stella to pose. Stella's parents (our daughter Emma and son-in-law Toby Tennant), brother Eddie, sister Isabel with her two-year-old baby, Rosa, Andrew and myself were all brought into the 'shoot', as well as another granddaughter, Jasmine Cavendish, and our dogs.

The teamwork of Bruce's assistants was fascinating to watch. They seemed to sense when he needed them and surrounded him with all he required – one holding the silver umbrella to shade the lens, others with extra cameras changing films at top speed. Joe McKenna, the stylist in charge of how the clothes, shoes and hats looked on Stella (who is as much at home in the lambing sheds of her father's farm in Scotland as she is on the catwalks of Paris, Milan and New York), is a master of his craft.

I have kept a few clothes I bought in Paris in the late 1950s and I showed them to Joe and his assistants. I had no idea they would be so interested. Forty-year-old Lanvin, Dior and Balmain garments were admired like Old Master paintings. They even photographed the labels as works of art in themselves.

The shape of 1950s coats and dresses has come back into fashion, as inevitably happens if you keep clothes long enough. So I was persuaded to put on one or two, while Stella wore the latest models. I am afraid the fifty-one-year difference in our ages was very apparent, but the Lanvin coat I wore at Ascot in 1959 compared well with Stella's new one by Prada. Bruce made me wear a red satin Balmain ball dress of 1960 – beautiful, certainly, but out of place at even the grandest entertainment now – to feed my chickens. The iron spoon and tin bucket were a huge contrast to the exquisite satin.

I have seldom met such a charming group of people – so hard-working, oblivious of the long hours, dedicated to their profession and to Bruce himself, who is a shining star. We were all very sad when the trunks were packed, the troupe left and the nursery was quiet again.

✢

Stella also wrote down her recollections of that weekend.

The floor outside the nursery at Chatsworth is covered in ancient lino-leum. It has a warmth and a particular smell that always remind me of when I was young, especially the excitement of arriving for Christmas. However, I wasn't opening presents last time I visited. I was there for a fashion shoot with Bruce and his team, along with all my family. It was strange to wander through those familiar rooms and find them full of alien clothes, shoes, bags and all kinds of accessories; even stranger to think that these were the same rooms that my sister Izzy and I had roller-skated wildly round as children.

My family was amazed by the scale of the shoot, which surpassed all their expectations. The weekend was a new experience for me too – intro-ducing my family to fashion and fashion to my family. Not only did my family get an unusual insight into what my work involves, but the role reversals were hysterical – my brother in Prada! Mum in Blahnik shoes! I've never seen her in anything other than gardening trousers or knee-length tweed. Fortunately, Joe skilfully managed to put her in outfits that suited her and in which she felt comfortable.

Granny, on the other hand, has a fantastic collection of clothes. (Now that the 1950s look is back in, she is in serious danger of having her ward-robe raided by her granddaughters.) I was amused when some of the shoot rubbed off on her and, having looked through Joe's wardrobe, she has placed an order for a Helmut Lang suit. Dad isn't male-model sample size, so no orders there, but Mum's getting some Manolos for Christmas.

As well as the fun and peculiar buzz of doing a fashion shoot with my family, it will be invaluable for us to have the pictures. In The Pursuit of Love, *my great-aunt Nancy compared such family portraits to flies held in the amber of the moment . . .*

⁂

In September 2006, another famous photographer worked at Chatsworth for a day: Mario Testino, a great friend of Stella. He took the pictures at her wedding in 1999, when she married his erstwhile assistant, David Lasnet, in the Scottish Borders on a May day of freezing cold and biting wind. The French guests had come dressed for summer and rued the choice, but it was the happiest day for all concerned.

Mario Testino, like Bruce Weber, is one of those all-time charmers who has the knack of making his subjects feel happy and at home in whatever outlandish garments the magazine decrees. He seemed to take a fancy to Chatsworth, which fired his enthusiasm and produced some memorable photographs for *Vogue*'s ninetieth anniversary issue. I described his visit in a letter to Paddy Leigh Fermor later that month.

So one Mario Testino, famous photographer, came in a helicopter with a crew of makeup, hairdresser, 'fashion editor' etc from London.

I've got a really beautiful dress, grand evening, given me by Oscar de la Renta, so that was my kit. They bound Stella's legs, up to where they join her body, in tartan. A Union Jack flag hung from her waist & her top was what my father would have called meaningless.

Hair skewbald/piebald, all colours & stuck up in bits. THEN they produced 'shoes' with 6 inch heels. More stilts – she could hardly put one foot in front of the other, wobbling & toppling, and being 6′ tall she turned into 6′ 6″.

(I forgot to say to Paddy, a prop was a big toy lamb, legs dangling as though dead.)

We looked just like that Grandville drawing of a giraffe dancing with a little monkey. I was the monkey.

Fashion is as queer as folks.

July 1995

ROMNEY MARSH AND OTHER CHURCHES

One of the great charms of England is the variety of country. You drive fifty miles and find yourself in a different world: different voices, landscapes, soil, breeds of sheep and, most noticeable, different buildings. But one feature is constant throughout the towns and villages of every county, and that is the churches and cathedrals. Not constant in date, shape, make or style but in the fact that they are there and, until not so long ago, that their towers or spires were the tallest buildings in the landscape, drawing attention to themselves as landmarks and proclaiming their importance to locals and travellers alike.

It is difficult to decide on a favourite. For myself, I so much prefer English churches to the more theatrical and dusty European ones, however magnificent their architecture. I so agree with the English nanny who was taken with her charges to Chartres Cathedral and, when they came out into the fresh air so beloved by nannies, was asked what she thought of it: 'Well, it's a bad light for sewing in there.'

The construction of these buildings seems nothing short of miraculous. Who designed them? How many people worked on them and for how long? How was it done? How and where did they get the stone? And WHY? If we ponder these questions of village churches, what about cathedrals? Ely, which makes you gasp when you walk in and look up, or Wells with its magical Chapter House stairs. In some cases the answers to these questions are known – the dates, a few facts, such as the stone having been brought from Caen in France, it being comparatively easy to bring by sea. *Easy?* Well, it depends on what you mean by easy.

What is difficult to evaluate today, and can hardly be imagined, is the faith that inspired these incredible buildings. It is this that gives them an indefinable sense of wonder. I find it intensely moving to go into a church alone, to allow the atmosphere to overwhelm me and take me for a few minutes back into the past, to drink in the peace which such an atmosphere brings. It eases the mind and puts the bothers of everyday life into perspective.

The fourteen churches that come under the Romney Marsh Churches Trust are truly amazing, from the smallest – St Thomas Becket, Fairfield, with its inspired white-painted pews, edged in black, that are unlike any other church interior – to the Cathedral of the Marsh, the vast St George at Ivychurch, which must have been too big for the community it served even seven centuries ago. Why that size? The churches are spread around Rye, on the wetlands that support the Romney Marsh sheep (which make such good eating). In our crowded country, the area is a haven of peace; the ancient roads that thread their way past dykes and through flood plains are emptier than those of the remote Peak District two hundred miles north.

Someone sent me a newspaper cutting with an article about walking on Romney Marsh next to an article about walking in Derbyshire. What caught my eye was the grumble of the Marsh walker when he came to a ploughed field on his way to a church, and sticky grey earth piled on to his boots, thus inconveniencing him. More space was given to the mud on his boots than to his description of the church. I wonder how he would have reacted to the slightly bigger inconveniences which must have beset the builders and congregations of centuries ago.

I think it is simpler when you're old. I suppose long experience of the trivia of life makes one glad to be able to absorb the other sort of experiences, to be able to consider the wonder of buildings, of their builders, of the generations of preachers and lay people who guarded their sanctity and the centuries of prayer that have left their mark. How else can you explain what one feels?

When my sisters and I were children at Asthall, in Oxfordshire, the churchyard was almost in our garden. Although we weren't allowed to, we used to watch the funerals from the nursery window, fascinated. My sister Jessica and I fell into a newly dug grave once and our much older sister Nancy pronounced fearful bad luck on us for the rest of our lives. We must have driven the grown-ups mad, writing Greta Garbo and Maurice Chevalier in the church visitors' book. I've since read in John Piper's brilliant piece in the 1937 *Shell Guide to Oxfordshire* that 'the inside of Asthall Church is like a church furnisher's catalogue', and that 'there is a fourteenth-century canopied effigy of Lady Joan de Cornwall'. All very fine but lost on me at the age of six.

Later we moved to Swinbrook, a few miles from Asthall, still on the River Windrush. It has a church of great beauty which contains the amazing early seventeenth-century monuments of the Fettiplace family – stone men lying full-length on their sides, heads supported on their hands, elbows resting on stone pillows – described by John Piper as 'intelligent, wicked looking former lords of the village, lying on slabs like proud sturgeon in enormous wall tombs'.

There is also a big wooden board in the church at Swinbrook with the Ten Commandments painted in a beautiful script. Another board announces that in 1617, £10 15s 9d was left by a benefactor with instructions that the income from this sum be used for 'charitable purposes' for the poor of the parish. But the last sentence dashes all hopes for the unlucky poor. 'This money is now lost,' it states.

My father used to take the collection at services and would pass round the plate twice to our aunt, his penniless sister. This happened every Sunday and the second time round she used to frown at him. He would remain in front of her looking hopeful until she slapped his hand, which set us off on the peculiar agony of church giggles.

I suppose there is no church in the country that does not have a memorial to its sons killed in the two world wars. Sometimes whole families of young men are listed as having died. If one of several brothers survived the Great War to father a son, as like as not that son's name will be among the dead of the last war. These memorials set one wondering what this country would be like now had those wonderful people, many of them just boys when they died, survived.

We know that regular congregations of churchgoers are getting smaller (except, I must say, at our village church in Derbyshire where I believe the church is full for two reasons: firstly, because the vicar is loved and, secondly, because he uses the 1662 Prayer Book and King James Version of the Bible). But the milestones of life – christenings, weddings and funerals – are still celebrated in church. The people who do not go regularly to church but who *use* it, as it were, for these purposes take it for granted that it will be there when they need it and would be dismayed if it suddenly wasn't.

Even more surprising are the memorial services to people who made a point of *not* going to church all through their adult lives. Yet when they die their relations feel they must arrange a memorial service in church. There seems to be a deep necessity for saying the final goodbye in the safety and sanctity of such surroundings. Humans have a need for a faith in which they can immerse themselves, even for a short time, to celebrate or to mourn. When the mind is all over the place, the Church provides something ancient and lasting – a feeling of stability that nothing else can equal.

1996

123

SASSOON: THE WORLDS OF PHILIP
AND SYBIL

by Peter Stansky

Describing these two shining stars from the East who arrived in
this country apparently by divine providence, Peter Stansky has
quoted from their many friends. Luckily the people who knew
the Sassoons were famous themselves, so their thoughts are in
diaries and memoirs from before the First World War until
Sybil's death, aged ninety-six, in 1989.

Their ancestors were devout Jews from Baghdad who settled
in Bombay, traders who dealt in opium and skins. Six Sassoon
brothers arrived in England in 1858 and immediately made their
mark. Abdullah, soon to be Albert, was the first Jew to receive
an honorary Freedom of the City of London and was made a
baronet in 1880 as reward for good works. Albert's son, Edward,
married Aline de Rothschild and so the fortunes of the two
great Jewish families were joined and, in due course, came to
their children: Philip, born in 1888, and Sybil, six years younger.
Their exotic background stayed with them for all to see and
enjoy. They were at the core of what used to be called 'society'
and set a standard of luxury and elegance slightly foreign to the
old English families, who delighted in glimpses of a glamorous
way of life which they did not go in for themselves.

Philip went to Eton. When his house was on fire he poured a
bucket of eau de cologne on the floor of his room. Osbert Sitwell
was his fag so presumably had to clean up the mess. In 1912, he
became the youngest MP (aged twenty-four) winning Hythe,

a seat he held for twenty-seven years. He was ADC to General Haig from 1915. Eyebrows were raised about a man of his age being safely on the staff while his contemporaries of promise were cannon fodder. After the war he passed, apparently effortlessly, as parliamentary private secretary to Haig's loathed Lloyd George, a chameleon-like feat. He served both masters loyally.

At Trent Park north of London, at Port Lympne overlooking Romney Marsh in Kent and at 25 Park Lane, he lavishly entertained politicians of all persuasions, the royal family, writers, actors, musicians and artists, from Charlie Chaplin to the Prince of Wales – via the Sitwells, John Singer Sargent, T. E. Lawrence, Lytton Strachey and Noël Coward – to Mr and Mrs Baldwin and Lloyd George and his mistress. All were delighted to luxuriate in his company and eat his superb food, surrounded by works of art shown to me later by Sybil with the words, 'These were my brother Philip's things, they are the best of their kind.'

In 1924, his love of beauty led him to reface the sombre-looking Trent Park with rose-coloured bricks from the demolished Devonshire House, and to people it with statues from Stowe. At Lympne he took his guests up for a spin in his own aeroplane, to the fish market in Folkestone (in his constituency) where the fishmongers crowded round him; then polo, followed by a swim in the sea and a memorable dinner. His energy was frenetic.

The red-headed radical Labour MP Ellen Wilkinson recorded his arrival in the House of Commons, with 'that fascinating lisp of his', and continued, 'If he would tuck up his legs and sit on the Big Table behind the Mace, with one finely carved hand on each brass box, he would make an appropriate Eastern altar-piece.' In the 1930s, his service in the air ministry was dear to his heart, since he was himself an aviator. It was followed by the perfect appointment for him – the Office of Works.

Philip, the perfectionist, loved life and made the most of his glittering opportunities. In Rome he had audiences with the Pope, Mussolini and the King; he preferred the exquisitely dressed Pope's 'white flannel and sapphire'. His Holiness 'kept me over an hour and rocked with laughter . . . so thankful to be with a heathen & not to talk *Shop.*' But in spite of the trappings, Philip, described so often as 'oriental', remained an exotic outsider – solitary in his invited crowd.

His adored Sybil ('she is the most charming person in the world. I love her so much. I can never marry, she sets me too dizzy a standard') must have made the stuffy 'society' of 1913 sit up when she married Lord Rocksavage to become mistress (and saviour) of Houghton Hall, from 1919 until her death.

In both world wars Sybil held high office in the Wrens. Years later I watched her, well over eighty, pulling on miserably thin blue gumboots for a day's shooting on the frozen Norfolk plough. 'Naval issue,' she said, proudly. She was the best woman shot I ever saw, as easily in tune with the Houghton keepers as with the aesthetes of Kensington Palace Gardens, the Cholmondeleys' London house. Her fifty-five-year marriage to the handsome Rock Cholmondeley, Lord Great Chamberlain, was a total success. She had a parade of would-be lovers, including Sir William Orpen ('Old Orps' as she called him), but Rock, her children and Houghton were the solid background of this fascinating creature who spread her aura over all lucky enough to know her.

If you want to escape from war, sex and shopping, join Philip and Sybil on their magic carpet and read this book.

April 2003

ANIMAL PORTRAITS

I wish James Lynch, a living Somerset artist whose work I love, would turn his attention to poultry. His three gouache pigs – a Gloucester Old Spot, a Middle White with fat cheeks and squashed snout, and a sleeping Tamworth – have been joined more recently by a Hereford bull in my bedroom at Bolton Abbey in Yorkshire.

Dog paintings are now high fashion. There is a goodly number at Chatsworth as the Bachelor (6th) Duke of Devonshire adored his dogs and had several of them painted, some by Sir Edwin Landseer. These paintings are a continual joy to me. One shows the duke's Sussex spaniel, Tawney, by the Colosseum in Rome – said by his owner to be Tawney's favourite resort.

I have added to my collection by buying at Bonhams' 'Dogs in Art' sale, which takes place every January. Some of these pictures are in our Devonshire Arms Hotel at Bolton Abbey, where one of the sitting rooms is called the Dog Lounge. There is a pair of eager old-fashioned fox terriers, their studded leather collars giving away their date. The regulars seem to like them as much as I do.

I am a sucker for a sheep or a Shire horse. I remember Shires at work when I was a child. The smell of the leather harness mixed with that of sweat and new hay, and the feel of their coarse manes and tails, are such a part of my childhood that I delight in their likenesses now. I came across the crudely painted portraits of two turn-of-the-century beauties: *Ditchford Princess* and *Lockinge Bay Leaf*, with their irresistible manes and forms, standing four-square in their Warwickshire yard, a feathered leg at each corner.

And then there's the work of Lucy Kemp-Welch. Carthorses with hemp halters and huge, patient heads – these are all that the heart could desire. Lucy's illustrations for *Black Beauty* are extraordinarily moving, taking me back to being read aloud to and having to stop the reader when the tears came. I was lucky enough to get her watercolour, *In Double Harness*, which shows Black Beauty and his friend Ginger, every detail of the harness shining in pre-Great War perfection. In the same gallery hung its companion, *It Was Ginger* – the chestnut, her head hung low after long hours between the shafts of a hansom cab, has just been recognised by her old companion Black Beauty. Much as I would have loved to have both watercolours, *It Was Ginger* would have had to be kept out of sight, it is so sad. I wonder if anyone had the courage to buy it.

Pictures of sheep by Millet and Rosa Bonheur, which have been given to me as presents, complete my bedroom farmyard. A cheerful party to wake up to.

Surrounding myself with these things is a way of expressing my long-standing love of the subjects. Fancies change with the years but I am still delighted by them. The regrets are always for the opportunities that were missed.

February 1992

MOTORWAYS

In Derbyshire's bleak midwinter it is a comfort to come indoors for good at 4 p.m., out of the half light and off the sodden grass, knowing that – chickens fed and dogs, alas, dead – I need not go out again till morning. Staring into the fire and wondering what next, I read a masterly review of a best-selling book on commas (name too difficult to remember). It set off thoughts of words and how oddly they are used or misused.

Motorways, part of everyday life for car owners and lorry drivers, have a language of their own, invented by whom I do not know. Such roads are wider and faster (until bunged up) than little roads, but it would be easier, especially for foreigners, if their vocabulary were the same.

The part you drive on is called the 'carriageway'. This is a misnomer because carriages are not allowed to use it. Nevertheless, carriageway is repeated *ad infinitum* down the length of the three-car-wide tarmac. Roadworks are part of the fun of a long drive, making little diversions from the dull old slog. After you have wriggled sideways, guided by cones standing shoulder to shoulder, and faced oncoming traffic uncomfortably close for several miles, you are ordered to 'rejoin the carriageway'.

You begin to wonder if you will meet a four-in-hand, the coachman sitting high up in his many-tiered cape, top-hatted men travelling outside and crinolined ladies inside. At the service station there is a special place allocated to them clearly signed

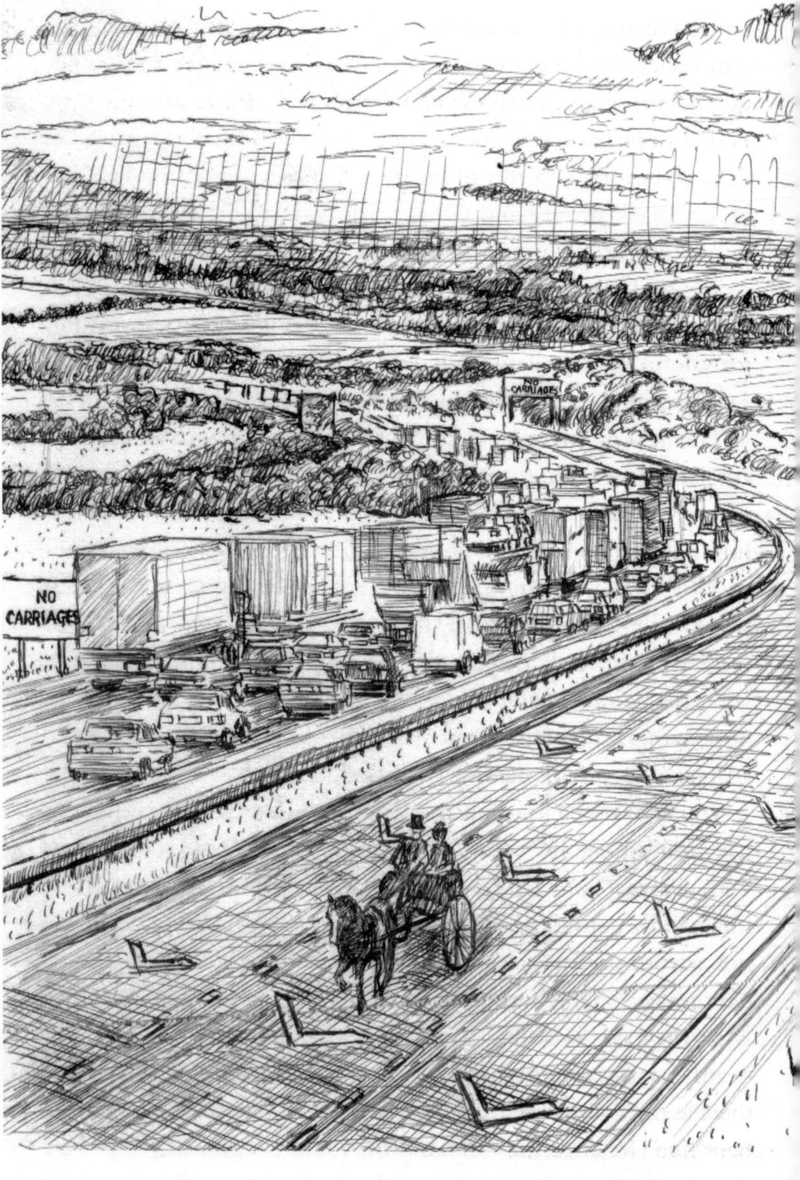
NO CARRIAGES
NO CARRIAGES

'Coaches Only'. Four fresh horses await the express coach to take it to the next stage. They are put to as in a scene painted by James Pollard, a barking terrier prancing round their feet in the atmosphere of excitement as the horses are changed in double-quick time, like the tyres on a Formula One car at a pit stop. Perhaps a phaeton will appear, one of those C-spring creations of delicate beauty, or a pair of Norfolk Trotters drawing a shooting brake. Black Beauty and Ginger trot past Junction 29, followed by Victorias and hansom cabs. Hackneys and Cleveland Bays are recognised as the elite of draught animals, while honest van-ners pull vehicles with drop sides that provide all kinds of wares for sale in neighbouring villages. But this is all imagination as carriages are not allowed on the carriageway.

The next words to learn are 'hard shoulder'. This is an import-ant part of the road, running parallel to the carriageway but a sort of poor relation. It is meant to be a place to stop in an emergency. It is indeed hard but I can't understand where the shoulder comes in. If it were a soft shoulder you could at least cry on it, which would help when in despair. It is no good leaning on this sort of shoulder as the police will move you on. If you lean long enough you risk being sectioned. Don't try to sleep there. In spite of notices that crop up frequently saying 'Tiredness Can Kill – Take a Break', sleeping is against the rules.

You will be picking up the language quite well by now, but just wait. Suddenly a sign introduces another word, 'chevrons', with 'Watch Your Distance – Keep Two Chevrons Apart'. It is followed by upside-down Vs painted on the road. Chevrons is not a word used every day so you stop on the hard shoulder to get the dictionary from the bowels of the boot in order to know what they are on about. The *Shorter Oxford* says a chevron is 'a beam or rafter; especially in plural, the couples of the roof which meet at the ridge; a charge on the escutcheon, consisting of a bar bent like two meeting rafters, thus Λ; a distinguishing mark on the sleeve of a non-commissioned officer, policeman'.

Those who are not builders by trade may hesitate for a moment or two while they imagine how the beams and rafters of a roof meet. Having assimilated this (not too difficult but it does distract you from keeping your distance), you are then faced with the mysterious language of heraldry. 'A charge on the escutcheon' might be crystal clear to the compilers of *Burke's Peerage* but rather obscure to the majority of lorry drivers. People over eighty who lived through the war may remember the marks like meeting rafters (or a charge on the escutcheon) worn on the sleeve of a non-commissioned officer – three for a sergeant, two for a corporal and one for a lance corporal – but the vast majority of the population have never seen them.

So that is the language of the motorway. I am thankful there are no hard shoulders or chevrons on the way to Bakewell and that the road is not a carriageway. Should you wish to travel by horse and cart you can.

MEMORIAL SERVICES

Memorial services have swum into fashion. I don't know why because most of those remembered (with some notable exceptions) did not go into a church after they grew up, except possibly for their first wedding. The reason may be that, as death is against the rules now, the sight of a coffin at a real funeral is too much for the sensitive.

These gatherings used to be arranged only for prime ministers or for men who had spent their lives in public service. Now they happen for every Tom, Dick and Harry, and have spread to Thomasina, Ricardia and Harriet. They cause a lot of anxiety. There is doubt as to whether you should go to the funeral, which is sometimes for family only but is apt to include some friends, or wait for the inevitable memorial, or both. Do you count as a great enough friend to intrude on family-only grief or not?

I have never been to a memorial service that has reminded me of the deceased. They seem to be an exercise in social behaviour, the congregation meeting out of duty in the hopes of pleasing relations rather than from a wish to bring back the memory of the person whose name is on the service sheet. Often as not the officiating clergyman does not know the person but has to carry on as if he did and put on the sad face learned for such occasions at his theological college. The one who did know Harry/Harriet is the unhappy victim chosen by the family to give an address. For weeks this friend has struggled with what to say, how honest to be, or whether he should just deliver a eulogy and leave the intimates to think about what the deceased was really like. If the speaker makes jokes it can be acutely embarrassing. If he does not, there is no relief from the solemnity and he may leave out an important part of his subject's character.

A grandchild, deeply fond of the departed and overcome by the occasion, the surroundings and the unaccustomed lectern, reads. Watching and listening can be as painful for the congregation as it is for the performer. Sometimes there are several readings. 'Jabberwocky' is fashionable just now. The old and deaf can hardly believe what is left of their ears.

Then there is the music. It has been chosen with great care by the nearest and dearest, and includes an anthem, which is a splendid chance for the little boys in the choir to show their skill and sing the high notes before their voices break. The anthem ensures you are in for a lengthy sit. There is no knowing how long it will last. The dangerous word is 'Alleluia', which is spun out far longer than you can imagine possible when you see it written down. What is more, it is repeated again and again. 'Lo' can rattle on a bit, but 'O' is the worst offender. Even when it has dropped its 'h' this single letter goes on and on, up high, down low, fast, slow, back to where it started, then up and down once more till you wonder what can ever stop it. In spite of the anthem, the service eventually comes to an end and you meet the family and friends on the steps of the church. 'That was very beautiful,' you hear yourself say, when you are thinking of lunch or the train.

Compare it to the burial service of the 1662 Prayer Book in Archbishop Cranmer's magnificent language, moving and comforting – 'For we brought nothing into this world, and it is certain we can carry nothing out' – and the time-honoured ceremony ending in the churchyard, accompanied by sun, wind, rain or snow – 'all ye works of the Lord'. We are reminded that golden lads and girls and chimney sweepers, and those of us in between, are not immortal. The coffin is lowered into the grave accompanied by the final farewell, 'Man that is born of a woman hath but a short time to live, and is full of misery. He cometh, and is cut down, like a flower; he fleeth as it were a shadow, and never continueth in one stay.'

Isn't that good enough? Please, no memorial service.

OFTOF

We constantly read about the organisations that are meant to keep things straight for the benefit of those who use the relevant industries. OFCOM covers communications; OFGEM gas and electricity (but not jewellery); OFWAT, well, water of course; the aptly named OFRAIL; OFT, poetic for the Office of Fair Trading; and OPRA, nothing to do with music, pensions more likely.

Now we come to the latest and most far-reaching of all the OFs – OFTOF. The idea is to ensure that Old Etonians looking for work are seen off before getting to the interview stage. OFTOF will have already succeeded in blocking their progress to Oxford or Cambridge. Sometimes, in spite of this obstacle, the lads are accepted for an interview by a prospective employer. Then the pantomime begins.

It is against the rules to ask a prospective employee what colour they are, if they are married, have children or if they are a terrorist, yet it is allowed to ask if they've been to school and even to narrow it down and ask which school. Narkover* is all right, of course, and Fettes, but if the word Eton should slip out, OFTOF is summoned immediately and the candidate is told to push off and on no account to reapply for the job under another name because the ghastly truth will out.

The OFTOF man may himself be a public schoolboy, even an Old Etonian, and be up to all the ruses learnt there. He will also know of the despairing parents who have scraped and saved to pay for their lad to get a good education, have sweated down the M4 for various school celebrations for five years only to realise that OFTOF has the whip hand and there is no hope of the boy finding gainful employment.

February 2004

* Narkover, the school in Beachcomber's *Daily Express* 'By The Way' column, specialised in gambling, racing and extortion.

Since this article was published, the OFTOF officials seem to be slipping as one or two top jobs have been landed by Old Etonians. What next?

CONSERVATIVE?

How contrary the British people are and how we hate change.

When British Rail was just British Rail it was a joke, like mothers-in-law and piles. Now that it is 'threatened' with privatisation, it has suddenly blossomed into a loved institution bordering on heritage. Flowers have appeared on platforms and stations have been repainted as they were in the olden days. One London terminus even has a porter. Suddenly it must no longer be laughed at or, if it is, it must be in the indulgent way of a parent with a favourite child. Snow and autumn leaves on the line are excused as something to do with the environment and therefore sacrosanct.

It is the same with the Health Service and Education. They were hopeless, people said, until their ministers tried to improve them. Now the cry is, leave our hospitals alone and don't interfere with the schools.

Who says we are not conservative?

September 1993

DEBATE AT THE CAMBRIDGE UNION

In autumn 2003, to his surprise and delight, Andrew received an invitation from the president of the Cambridge Union to take part in a debate. He accepted without hesitation. The rather curious motion was: 'This house would rather be an aristocrat than a democrat'. He was asked to speak for the aristocrats. The old warhorse in him smelt an agreeable battle ahead.

Years ago, he had taken part in another debate at the Union and remembered the atmosphere as antagonistic – to say the least – towards someone like him and he expected to find the same again only with knobs on. Imagine his surprise when the president wrote with the final arrangements – times for drinks and dinner, and dress *black tie*. That such an outfit should have shaken off its mothballs and re-emerged at a student debate was a huge surprise. Where are the jeans of yesteryear? What has precipitated such a change? Instead of missiles – from soggy bread-rolls indoors to more serious weaponry in the street – he found nothing but good manners and a student dinner-companion of such charm he has been talking about her ever since.

You will be surprised to hear that the motion was carried by the democrats, the poor old aristocrats biting the dust as usual. Andrew abstained. I am told by someone who was there that when he finished speaking the applause was loud and prolonged.

'So what did you say?' I asked. 'Oh, I can't remember.' But the audience had laughed – and that was the point.

February 2004

CHANGING LANGUAGE

In 1994 I wrote a piece for *Country Life* about changes in our language on rural matters: country turning into countryside, hedges into hedgerows, bogs into wetlands and so on. Weather forecasters have changed the age-old Scottish 'hills' of poets, shepherds and sportsmen into 'mountains'. 'Home is the hunter from the mountain'? Surely not. The new words are longer and sound more important but the additions are unnecessary for meaning.

We know that language changes. Sixty years on, who would say *Great Scott, By Jove, vamp, scram, mannequin, blighter, shut-eye, copper* (or *Bobby* for that matter)? Many would not even know what the words mean. *Swank, spiffing, pansy* and *top-hole* have gone with the wind. So have those dressing-table necessities *cold cream* and *vanishing cream*. *Capital, conked out* and *topping* have also disappeared. Cars don't have *chokes* any more (they hardly have gears and their windows have given up winding down).

Shoot used to mean a cheery gathering of friends bent on a day's sport. If pheasants are the quarry, it will take place during the darkest season of the year; if partridges, it is likely to be in October; if it's in August, you'll be on a grouse moor. But whatever the weather, you go. Today a *shoot* can mean a crowd of curiously dressed young men and women, one of whom is king of the camera. In spite of being armed with huge silver umbrellas they don't go out in the rain, so in this part of England there is a lot of waiting about. It makes for frayed tempers as there is a deadline to be met for the fashion magazines. Nothing could be more different from the other kind of *shoot*.

A *stalker* was, and still is, a man whose name is likely to begin with Mc. He wears a fore-and-aft hat and crawls on his stomach over bog and rock, spying for a stag, and he is often in charge of an amateur behind a rifle. Today he is also someone who takes a fancy to (usually) a woman and can actually be arrested for his trouble. *Stalking* is now a criminal offence.

There is a new vocabulary spawned by technology, most of it as ugly as *blog*. A *web* is nothing to do with spiders (or lies) and is used a thousand times a day by all. The same goes for *net*.

Technology apart, change gallops on. Words are as much driven by fashion as are hats. The chosen ones are done to death till they lose their impact. *Icon*, for instance. *Icons* are everywhere, chiefly actors and actresses or television people. *Iconic* describes anything desirable till he, she or it falls from grace because of a scandal to do with money or sex (though the latter sometimes adds to the fascination). The dictionary says an *icon* is 'a representation of some sacred personage, itself regarded as sacred, and honoured with a relative worship'. I suppose this is how those people and objects are seen, but everyday use has devalued the word and no doubt we shall soon hear of a new one to describe 'anything venerated or uncritically admired'.

Consumer is a funny one. It seems we are all *consumers* not just of food and drink, which you can understand because we have to consume them to stay alive, but of everything we buy. How can you *consume* a sofa? Or a string of pearls, a car or a cruise? Perhaps an obese person could open a vast mouth and cram in a piano or two before sending for the fire brigade to recover them, but it is unlikely. We must all give it some thought. Meanwhile lunch is ready and I will *consume* it.

Market place and *workshop* worry me. I think of the former as where Bakewell Market happens every Monday – cattle and sheep at one end and at the other a thrilling mixture of kitchen gadgets, stuff by the yard, household goods, clothes, fruit and veg, all under dripping canvas and cheaper than in the shops – cheerful bargains on every stall. I am wrong. *Market place* applies to where anything is bought and sold, including the antics of City traders in their shirtsleeves yelling at each other down telephones without a cow or sheep in sight – and certainly not in mind.

Surely a *workshop* is a shed where carpenters in aprons and other talented men make something. Saws, hammers and chisels hang in neat patterns on the wall and the floor is deep in wood shavings and sawdust. But the word has been bagged by the ubiquitous actors and actresses who speak of a *theatre workshop* – the next best thing to an oxymoron, to my mind. There are theatres and there are workshops but they don't go together.

An *issue* is as common as an *icon* and is beginning to replace a *problem*. I don't like the sound of it, conjuring up as it does the woman in the Bible with an *issue of blood*. Politicians are very keen on them. There is usually more than one and they can't make up their minds as to what to do with them. They spin out the time, unresolved, till a more urgent *issue* comes along, which is almost at once.

You can't hide behind *transparency* because you can see through it. Mr Blair was as *transparent* as they come and full of *issues* which you could also see through. Everything has to go through a *process*. A *peace process* is the favourite, perhaps because there are so many wars. The United States is enduring an *electoral process* and I am about to get out of bed and follow a *dressing process*. Quite a business and one that involves a *strategy* as well. Generals used to be the ones for that, conducting a campaign and manoeuvring an army. Now *strategy* is used instead of 'plan', I suppose because it sounds better, more urgent, with a warlike ring to it.

Don't forget *scenario*. Back to the theatre: 'An outline of a dramatic work scene by scene', says the dictionary. It is dangerously close to *strategy*, both words used to enliven dull sentences and brighten up dull lives by constant reference to the stage. If you don't look out you'll be back in that *theatre workshop* where you can deal with *strategic scenarios* in the company of *icons*.

When I was a shopkeeper I was forever *sourcing* things. Unwittingly, though; I thought I had just found them. The source of the Thames is there all right, mysterious and romantic, but it is quite different from trudging down the aisles of *Consumer Goods* at Trade Fairs, yet I was *sourcing* the day away on that ploy.

Rooms are *spaces*. You can't fill them with consumer goods because they must be minimalist, i.e. empty. A drawing room, once a withdrawing room, is no longer. It must be just a *space* – there is nowhere to withdraw to. It cannot be a *drawing space* because that is a studio, which has another meaning. The unhappy tenant of a studio is not a draughtsman but just a person who has been squashed into a very small *space* by a greedy landlord.

Bureaucrats love *putting things in place*. I think it means starting something – but that is often an *initiative*. So you put your *initiative in place*. This is after it has been vetted by a few committees, some planners and a panel of experts. The whole thing is soon forgotten. Even so, it could become an *issue* before you've had time to ask an *icon* to open it.

Watch out for *initiative*. Don't, whatever you do, use your own. You'll break the law and bring Health and Safety running. It is better to quash it before the *process* begins or you will be branded as a menace to society. The mere idea of doing anything without consulting consultants is too risky even for a risk assessor to *put in place* and *drive forward*. And a *road map*? Oh, PLEASE . . .

If you mind any of this, never fear, it will be all change soon and we can rest in peace.

DEPORTMENT

After spending a day in Oxford during term time, I have been wondering what has happened to deportment. Isn't it high time it was brought back as a compulsory class at school? I suppose there would be a riot and the Narkover-type pupils of today would knife the teacher before the lesson could begin.

If only the girls could see themselves in their expensive, creased jumble, slouching about, faces hidden by curtains of hair, compared to how they would look if they carried themselves like Edwardian beauties. There would come about a change which would cheer things up no end wherever young people congregate.

The girls are just as pretty as they always were but they go to amazing lengths to hide it. Yet they spend fortunes on make-up and tragic coverings, which can hardly be described as clothes.

I think they must be longing to sit on juries, for we are repeatedly told that anyone who is clean, tidy and stands up straight is objected to for jury service without further reason.

June 1986

CHRISTMAS AT CHATSWORTH

Little was made of Christmas at Chatsworth in the eighteenth and nineteenth centuries as, strangely enough, there were no Cavendish children there for nearly a hundred years. It all came to life early in the twentieth century when the newly refurbished theatre became the scene of home-made entertainment of the most sophisticated kind. Professional singers and amateur members of the week-long house parties sang and acted sketches, with King Edward VII and Queen Alexandra heading the guest list at the regular annual shoots of the 8th Duke of Devonshire and his German duchess. The audience was magnificently dressed and glittering in diamonds.

In 1908 Victor (9th Duke) and Evelyn arrived with their large family. In due course they had twenty-one grandchildren, who made the Christmases of the 1920s and 1930s memorable. The parents came with their maids and valets, the children with their nannies, grooms and ponies (they hunted with the High Peak Harriers on Boxing Day). Some of the nannies were keenly aware of the status of their charges. My sisters-in-law remember being told to sit on their luggage in a passage while their nanny demanded the best night-nursery, already occupied by Stuart cousins who had arrived earlier. On the insistence of Nanny, the cousins were ousted in favour of the preferred Cavendish girls.

Granny Evelyn had a famous cook, Mrs Tanner, who trained under Escoffier no less. She left books of receipts which show that the Christmas food was rich and rare – so were the menus, which seemed to go on for ever. The dining room, schoolroom and nursery all had different menus. The unlucky children had to eat the hateful bland food thought suitable for their ages. Even the Christmas puddings were made of different ingredients according to where they would be eaten. Those for the staff were mostly suet and breadcrumbs mixed with stout and milk, whereas Mrs Tanner's 'Best Christmas Pudding, Buckingham Palace receipt' included French plums, stoned raisins and half muscatels, plus half a bottle of brandy – underlining the great unfairness of life.

With my own family in Oxfordshire it was different. Seven of us children were a solid start. My mother gave a tea party for the Asthall and Swinbrook schoolchildren on Christmas Eve, with the parson as Father Christmas. She bought and wrapped a toy and a garment for each child and took infinite trouble over the list of ages and sexes. One year she settled on penknives for the boys. Today these innocents would find themselves in the police station.

Christmas Day routine never varied for us. Early-morning opening of stockings, church, undoing presents ('the festival of paper', my mother called it), lunch of turkey and a plum pudding with sixpences, bachelor's buttons and other anti-Health and Safety charms embedded in it, and, after dark, a card game so simple that the youngest and stupidest of the children (me) could play. Fancy dress in the evening – anything to hand was seized on. My sister Nancy was always the most imaginative. My father's only concession was to wear a red wig. He took the group photograph so was never in it. My mother must have been thankful when it was all over.

It starts in October now. The Chatsworth Farm Shop is packed with things to eat and people to buy them, its reputation having spread since its quiet start in 1976, when we had planning permission to sell only hunks of freezer meat. The hampers are sent

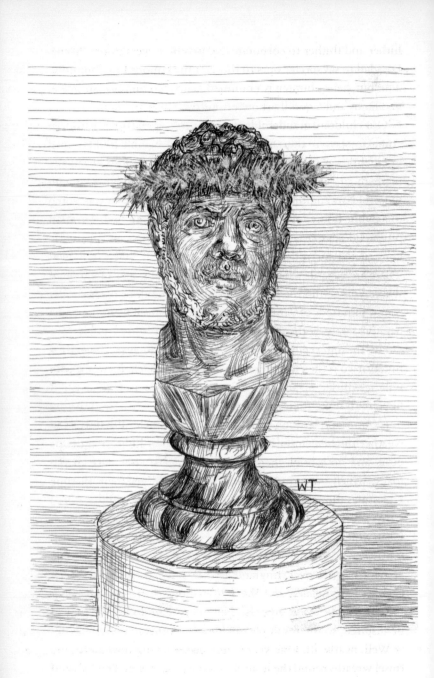

hither and thither to corporate and private buyers galore. Some, I'm glad to say, prefer ours to those of the famous London shops. The butchery counter is crammed with 745 turkeys, 50 geese, 400 hams and a goodly show of our own beef and lamb.

Our children, grandchildren and fourteen great-grandchildren come to stay in alternate years. It is odd having middle-aged grandchildren, and some of the greats are getting on. The change in them in two years is fascinating to see. The five-year-old, who told an enquiring schoolfriend last year that he was going to a public house for Christmas, will probably give a dissertation on Euclid next year when he is seven. Stone passages apparently constructed for roller-skating come in useful when it is wet. There are hazards which make it more exciting, like a long ramp where you get up the speed to crash into the door of the boiler room, hundreds of yards and two staircases away from the comparative safety of the nursery.

For the intervening Christmases come old (very) friends – ninety-two is the oldest this year – plus a wheelchair cousin who will be whirled up and down the corridors by a nine-year-old, I hope with some notion of safety.

It's no good sinking into a chair after lunch. Whatever the weather the hens must be fed. The midwinter light soon disappears and no sensible hen stays out of doors after dark or the foxes, which our government adores, would get their all-time Christmas dinner.

In 2001, the spectre of foot-and-mouth caused havoc at Chatsworth. Andrew suggested the house should stay open till Christmas to recoup the losses, and so it has remained. People come from all over England to see it decorated and lit by candles (yes, *candles*) and the house-shops turn into fairyland. No one from outside advises. The house staff do it and seem to be inspired, so the result pleases all who come.

Well, nearly all. One year I got a letter saying how awful the tinsel wreaths round the heads of Roman busts were ('tacky') and what frightful taste I have to allow such a travesty. So we can't please everyone, but I think Christmas without tinsel, however Roman the heads, would simply not be Christmas.

October 2005

THE FALL AND RISE OF THE STATELY HOME

by Peter Mandler

'Aristocracy', says the dictionary, means 'government of a state by its best citizens'. All over now – more's the pity – and the so-called aristocrat, now powerless, is hardly the word to describe the latter-day villains of this book. As builders of the stately homes, they started off quite well. Hatfield, Penshurst, Burghley, Haddon, Hardwick and Co. were all open to the public in the eighteenth century. Two hundred years later the railways brought big crowds and it was still considered the people's right to be shown round these houses, romanticised by the Victorians. Entry was free.

It was a shock when Lord Sackville, a crusty old chap who disliked his fellow men, closed Knole in the 1880s. There was a near-revolution in Sevenoaks where the tradespeople depended on the trippers. One or two owners began to charge to reduce numbers but it was the 4th Earl of Warwick who, in 1886, actually set about turning his castle into an asset rather than a liability. His family continued to do so till 1978, when they eventually succumbed to a tempting offer from Madame Tussaud.

Peter Mandler lumps owners together as if they were a breed of dog when, in fact, they are as individual as their houses. It is their problems and interests which are the same. The Lords Warwick get the publicity, but for one of them there are dozens of steady people who look after their inheritance, as well as carrying out endless local duties, which the author finds too boring to mention. The silent majority still *in situ* seem to me to have ridden out the storms of punitive taxes, recurring agricultural depressions, wars, pestilence and Lloyd's, with judgement and rectitude.

Mr Mandler seems to be unaware that the statelies have attendant cottages, farm roads and buildings, and endless outgoings that must be paid for, as well as the upkeep of the houses themselves. Pensions? Not mentioned. Forestry is deemed to be an asset. In all the years I have lived near trees they have been a constant drain on estate resources. The author often mentions, but fails to understand, the Englishman's deep-seated love of his land.

The unfortunate owners can't do right. If, like Lord Montagu, they try and make a go of the place, they are greedy. If they are forced by taxation to sell up, they are running away. If they sell what is loosely called a 'work of art' to pay for new lead on the roof, they are 'threatening the integrity of the house'. But if holes in the roof allow the Old Master drawings and rare books to get wet there is not much integrity left.

He is surprised that little was done about country houses in the 1940s. Had he been in England then, he would have noticed that the minds of government and owners were on other things. He might look at the names on war memorials in village churchyards – few landowning families were spared the deaths of men of military age.

In the 1950s, taste descended to a nadir and the author is right in saying that few English people wanted to live – and fewer wanted to work – in a big house. There has been a gradual change in attitude which has gained momentum in the last twenty years. Television programmes have sharpened people's interest in works of art, and concern for conservation of the best buildings and their contents is driven by 2,300,000 members of the National Trust.

The author can hardly bear it when things begin to look up for some owners but, alas, many houses are still vulnerable and will inevitably come on the market to be sold, and almost immediately resold when the buyers discover they don't fancy their new responsibilities and have bitten off more than they can chew.

Hoping for a word of encouragement in the summing up, I find French chateaux cited as an 'instructive comparison'. Oh PLEASE. You can't compare them. There are two basic differences between French and English attitudes to country houses. Frenchmen who have the choice would rather live in Paris than in the country, whereas the opposite holds here. The Code Napoléon has split up estates and emptied the chateaux of their contents, while primogeniture has been the saviour of what is left in this country – and a great deal is left.

The academic-eye view cites reasons for visiting houses as nostalgia and snobbism. Nowhere can I find the word 'beauty' to describe a house or garden, and I believe that to be the reason you and I enjoy seeing the wonders that are available to us. There are mistakes in facts and figures and little which is constructive but, living over the shop as it were, I read it with intense interest.

April 1997

COLD HOUSES

Anyone of my age is qualified to write about cold houses. Staying away in the 1930s for Pony Club dances before graduating to hunt balls taught me many a lesson in how to survive when the liberty bodice was overtaken by an off-the-shoulder evening dress.

Friends' parents usually made a big effort to warm the house on the evening of the entertainment but for some strange reason no one feels cold in his own house, besides which they always started too late. Beatrice Lillie's song, 'Oh, For a Night in the Ballroom' – 'fires in the bedroom at four' – said it all. The hostess, always an outdoor creature, was bound to be doing something with her dogs till the winter sun went down. The host was apt to be out hunting, so serious stoking didn't start till they got in.

The best moment was a hot bath before dinner. In a big house you might have quite a trek to reach this haven of warmth and if someone else got there before you it was bad luck. You had to retrace your steps down the draughty passage and face the fact that the hot water may have run out. Twice I suffered the cruellest cut of all: hot water gushing beautifully from its tap and empty silence from the cold tap. Nothing for it but, undressed and shivering and making a fog of steam, to leg it back to the bedroom, disappointed and unwashed.

If the dance was in another house, there was the drive in the car to contend with. No one under fifty remembers cars before heaters. My mother's car had wooden floorboards with big gaps between them so you could see the road rushing along under your feet. All the rugs in the world couldn't keep you warm.

Back to bed in the strange house to find perfectly ironed sheets, which are at once the coldest and the most luxurious things going. You slid between the icy, shining linen only to gather up your feet into a place made warmer by the rest of you.

But all that was long ago and at Chatsworth things aren't too bad. A new heating system was installed when we moved in and it works pretty well. Even so, the wind can penetrate huge old window frames which don't fit exactly. In September we go round with rolls of sticky brown paper to stop the gaps. When the front door is open and people with luggage dawdle, all our part of the house feels the blast so we've cut a small door out of the big one and you have to enter at speed. There are zones of intense cold, seldom visited in winter: the Sculpture Gallery, State Rooms and attics, where a closed-season search for forgotten furniture can feel colder than being out of doors.

Nothing is so bad for pictures painted on board, furniture and leather bindings as central heating; even the modest temperature of the rooms we live in does some damage. Humidifiers have been recommended but they are so hideous that I don't think I can bear to live with their sharp, white, metallic presence and horrible ceaseless noise. Anyway, they don't work. Perhaps a kettle or two perpetually on the boil would do the trick and be homelier.

No one has suggested air conditioning. There I draw the line. I prefer hit-or-miss English heating to waking up with swollen feet and fingers about to burst, like cows' udders at milking time, which happens after a night in an air-conditioned hotel. Or when in the tropics you need a fur coat to wear at dinner in an over-cooled restaurant.

After years of trial and error I've got my bedroom at Chatsworth about right, but there are the dogs to consider. When it was whippets, it seemed unkind to open the window at all. Then there was an old collie who would search for a cool spot, and for him the window had to be wide open. Labradors are accommodating as long as they aren't in a draught, and one slept under the bed. The springs made a noise that went through my head whenever he turned over.

It is far less risky to stay away in the winter now. Things have changed since Andrew and I spent two unforgettably cold January nights in an official house in Northern Ireland some years ago. We were given an enormous room with a single-bar electric fire (which I drew life-size in a letter to a sister). And yet you were expected to wear a décolleté dress in the evening.

Standards now get ever higher and when people talk of 'warm hospitality' I reckon they mean hospitality *is* warmth.

January 1987

RECOLLECTIONS OF DITCHLEY AND NANCY LANCASTER

I had a letter from Nancy suggesting I write what I remember of Ditchley. I said I would try. The next day came a postcard saying, 'I don't want a eulogy . . .'

After many years, does memory play you false? Do you look back on events, people and places in a slanted sort of way, slanted to summers being fine, friends always there, jokes, laughter, pleasure and entertainments galore, untouched by responsibility and living for the moment in a cheerful, hopeful sequence of exciting exploration? Perhaps you do, and perhaps it is lucky that adolescent discontent and the humdrum things which occupy most days are lost or are run together in a vague mist of recollection, and the special times remain, leapfrogging the rest. When I think of Ditchley all those years ago and the profound effect it had on me – and must have had on everyone who went there – it is impossible to write anything but a eulogy.

When I was a child we lived at Swinbrook, eleven or twelve miles away. I loved fox-hunting above all else and it was out hunting that I first saw Nancy. The meet of the Heythrop hounds was near our home, the unfashionable side of what was then an unfashionable hunt. The field consisted of people who lived in the Heythrop country, enlivened in term-time by wild undergraduates from Oxford riding unruly hirelings. Smart folk hunted in the shires. I can't imagine what Nancy was doing at Ford Wells on a Saturday.

I was trotting along on my dock-tailed pony when a big chestnut horse came thundering by. It was ridden on a loose rein by an elegant woman on a side-saddle wearing the Heythrop green livery, faultless top hat and veil – the smartest thing imaginable. 'Who is that?' I asked our old groom. 'Mrs Tree from Ditchley, on a blood 'orse.' He didn't have to tell me *that*. Later, when we passed the few horseboxes there were in those days, I saw her second horseman, a cockade in his top hat – something I had never seen before. I don't know who made the greater impression, I only know that I have never forgotten them.

I first went to Ditchley when I was sixteen or seventeen, having got to know Nancy's sons, Michael and Jeremy, out hunting. But I had seen the house before Nancy and her then husband Ronnie Tree bought it – empty and desolate, the park full of rabbits and sad white grass, at the time of the agricultural depression of the early 1930s. When Nancy and Ronnie arrived, it came to life and there they created perfection. On looking back, I realise that Ditchley taught me an invaluable lesson and that was to notice, to look, and try to absorb and remember what I saw that was beautiful. It was certainly the first time I became aware of such things. I suppose it was because of what Nancy gathered together under her roof, and the way she arranged the house. Whatever she touched had that hard-to-pin-down but instantly recognisable gift of *style*, arresting in its originality and satisfying to the spirit.

The house itself and its fixed decorations, together with much of the original furniture, was a wonderful start. But her genius (and that is no exaggeration) was her eye for colour, scale, objects and the dressing up of them, the stuffs the curtains are made of, their shapes and trimmings, the china, tablecloths, knives and forks; the things you see in all houses, but O the difference between Nancy's way with household necessities and anyone else's. Even the bathrooms were little works of art. Warm, panelled and carpeted, there were shelves of Chelsea china cauliflowers, cabbages, tulips and rabbits of exquisite quality. (A far cry from the cracked lino and icy draughts to which I was accustomed.) I had never seen such huge, square, down pillows as she went in for, nor the Porthault sheets decorated with carnations or trailing blue flowers of M. Porthault's imagination, and scalloped edges of the same colour. Nor the puffed-up eiderdowns covered in pale silk with tiny bows where a stitch held the cover in place. The tea tables, which came and went at the proper time, had no cloths but were painted brilliant Chinese red. Easy enough, anyone could have done that – but no one else did.

The rooms and their delectable contents were only part of the story. All that beauty could have been set up and people would have delighted in it, but the whole of Ditchley reflected the personality, the aura if you like, of Nancy herself. She was the star on the stage she created.

I can see her now, sitting bolt upright at the end of the dining-room table on one of the high-backed yellow chairs with Ronnie's initials embroidered on its cover, wearing something enviable with her own signature of a brilliant bit of colour somewhere, taking over the table so that people stopped to listen and laugh, making a comical mountain out of an ordinary molehill – a top-of-the-bill entertainer as well as a generous hostess.

The Trees were supported by a staff of servants no less talented at making their guests comfortable and happy than the hosts themselves. Mr Collins, the butler, was an extremely handsome man who was as polite to a seventeen-year-old girl as to a head of state. This invisible asset of perfect manners continued down to the housemaids, the kitchen staff, the grooms and the gamekeepers. These last were father and sons by the name of Starling, as neat and chirpy in their buttoned gaiters as the partridges they looked after. Cheerful Sunday morning visits to the chef and the stables were a pleasurable feature of staying at Ditchley.

In my mind's eye there is Mr Collins, tall and splendid in his tailcoat, piling coal on the hall fire on a Monday morning when most people in his profession would thankfully leave such a task till the next invasion of weekend guests. But at Ditchley you were made to feel they actually regretted your going. Rare enough. I have known two other houses where you have that feeling – Houghton with Sybil Cholmondeley at the helm and my sister Diana's Temple outside Paris.

Nancy and Ronnie were innovators in the garden, leaders of fashion outside as well as in. It was they who began the renaissance of old-fashioned roses, edging and designs in box, and so much else which has been copied *ad infinitum* in the last forty years and is so common now that you could be forgiven for forgetting who started it all.

After the war began and there was no petrol, I used to drive over from Swinbrook in a pony trap, fetching the pony out of the field and draping its second-hand harness over it to jog along the empty roads. On arrival the stud groom fetched it from the front door. Going home the next day the pony looked very different, shining all over, hooves dressed with oil and the harness and trap polished as never before.

When Winston Churchill used the house for weekends away from the bombing in London, I was delighted by Jeremy Tree's yawns and sighs and evident longing to go to bed when the PM started – and went on – talking till the early hours. (My own children did just the same years later when Harold Macmillan came to Chatsworth and talked till the cows came home.) At Ditchley we would have preferred to listen to Nancy.

I have no doubt that, as in every other family, you only had to scratch the surface to find worries, dramas and sorrows not far away. But such was the atmosphere created by the Trees and the magic of the place that, as a young girl, I found unalloyed pleasure in my visits there.

How short a time this oasis of perfection lasted. I count myself very lucky to have seen it. In my life I have been to many beautiful places and met many fascinating people but I have never seen the like of Ditchley and Nancy. 'I don't want a eulogy . . .' she said. Sorry, but how could it be otherwise?

HOME TO ROOST

I lived in the friendly palace that is Chatsworth for more than half my long life and, at eighty-five, I was the oldest person by far in that unusual house, where one of the many luxuries was that you never had to look at anything ugly because you were surrounded by the best of everything from four centuries. Chatsworth is unusual because of its size, beauty, fame, contents, garden, surroundings and staff, and the fact that it is visited by about 600,000 people every year. Under its roof is a kind of university of knowledge. Art historians, educationalists, cooks, needlewomen, accountants, plumbers, electricians, lodge porters, joiners, security guards, cleaners, retailers, lecturers, night watchmen, firemen, a photographer, a silver steward, a computer man and archivists mingle, their roles sometimes blurred and melting into the next profession. They make up an organisation unmatched in this country. That is the house I have left.

My new house was once the vicarage for the parish of Edensor, surrounded by a park wall and a ha-ha wide enough to deter the most athletic deer from invading the garden. The house is old and curiously constructed, having been altered many times since the eighteenth century. It has been enlarged, made smaller and enlarged again. We found windows in what is now an internal wall, and a stone gatepost, with a hinge for hanging a gate, at the bottom of the stairs – apparently holding up the first floor. Another surprise awaits upstairs where the landing and one of the bedrooms has a stone floor seven inches thick and therefore extremely heavy. No explanation has been discovered for these oddities. In another bedroom the builders removed some plaster from an internal wall to find it lined with reeds, the flowers still attached to the ends of the stalks. They have put a glass panel so you can see this pretty and practical kind of insulation.

Bits of house stick out at angles. The dining room and the bedroom above have three outside walls, causing the last tenant to retreat to a bedroom over the Aga. For me it is an unheard-of pleasure for the kitchen to be just two steps away and for it to be two steps the other way into the garden. At Chatsworth both destinations meant an expedition. Time to cancel the glossies and order the *Smallholder*.

One luxury has backfired badly. My new film star's bathroom has got a hand-held spray fed from the bath taps, something I have always wanted. Delighted, I tried it out. The beastly thing took control as if possessed of a devil and leapt about in my hand, soaking the much-too-pale film star's carpet and all else in its path with scalding water. I won't try that again.

Forty-six years and a month is not so long to stay in a house in these parts. There are a few ancients around who still live in the house where they were born. Nevertheless, nearly half a century produces a staggering accumulation of what my daughter calls 'glut' and decisions as to what to take from the quart jug to fit into the pint pot filled my waking hours and sometimes woke me when most people were sleeping.

A few precious things are lost in a move but many are found. Lurking unseen for years in a bookshelf was a Roxburghe Club volume, whose title I won't mention for fear of offending the donor. Given to Andrew by that elite company of bookworms, it was sitting there between *Fowls and How to Keep Them* and a slim volume to delight the heart of any teenage boy entitled *Studies in the Art of Ratcatching: A Manual for Schools*, published by John

Murray, no less, in 1891. I must ask the present bearer of that distinguished name if it was a best-seller.

At Chatsworth, clothes were hung far into a cupboard the size of an ordinary room in any normal house. Some French numbers of the 1950s and 1960s still hold their own in any company: quality incomparable; style timeless. One of the unwanted bedrooms in the Old Vicarage has become home for these beautiful garments. A granddaughter looked as if she had been poured into the simplest, best-cut, pitch-black evening dress – long sleeves, long skirt, no fuss, no decoration, made of some magic material between satin and thick silk. A dress to wear and to keep for her daughter now aged fifteen.

Trickier than pictures and clothes when it comes to a new home are ornaments: bits of china, stopped watches, presents from six-year-old grandchildren made with deepest concentration, hideous and easily broken but well remembered by the manufacturer and important for them to find still there. The boxes used by publishers sending books for our shops are invaluable at this point.

For weeks I felt like Edith Somerville, the Irish writer, who, aged eighty-eight, left her home of sixty years for a smaller house. In despair, she wailed to a nephew, 'Under everything there is something.' I pity people who have to move to the north of Scotland or Cornwall or, worse still, abroad. Being only a few hundred yards away, I can at least – like the Swiss Family Robinson – 'go back to the wreck' for a vital hammer or a pearl necklace left behind.

Decisions as to what to keep and what to throw are curiously wearing. Every scrap of paper, every ornament brings back its history with it. You pick them up and put them down, wondering. There is no doubt that throwing away is a kind of cleansing and you feel better afterwards. But you immediately want the thrown thing back and have to dig in the bonfire box. The drawer of my bedside table contained a horrid, ancient, floppy leather cover for a book. It held my mother's ABC Railway Guide and now encloses private papers from the lawyer. The ABC was a remarkable source of pre-war, pre-Beeching information to do with trains, their timetables of long ago – all, alas, irrelevant now – including the Early Closing Days for every town where there was a station.

My new house is spacious and sunny and has all the attributes beloved of estate agents. But the great thing about the Old Vicarage is its atmosphere. It is benign, serene, welcoming, good all through. Is the feeling left by the holy men who lived here? Do other Old Vics have the same legacy – intangible, but invaluable and very apparent? In 1838, the incumbent was Francis Hodgson, who went on to be Provost of Eton. He was a friend of Lord Byron and had his likeness in a marble head by Thorvaldsen. This somehow found its way to Chatsworth, but I am glad to say it is now back at the Old Vic. In 1856, the Reverend Joseph Hall was the vicar and remained in that office for fifty-one years. He must have known the place fairly well, a comforting thought in the restlessness of the 2000s. When the Reverend Harry O'Rorke arrived in 1908, the house was enlarged to accommodate his family of seven children and eight indoor servants. The widow of the last vicar to live here, Mrs Iola Symonds, is hale at ninety and often comes to see her old stamping ground. She had twenty-two rooms to look after. I have planted a tulip tree in the middle of her tennis court, which makes me feel guilty of desecrating the old playground.

The old vicars lived well here. The garden and outbuildings cover nearly two acres. A table to seat twenty would easily go into the dining room. There were fourteen bedrooms till 1972 when, wisely, the house was split to become the first semi-detached Old Vicarage in the country. There it has remained and I am the lucky tenant of what could be described as a rambling family home. The view to the west is lovely and gloomy. It reminds me of a hymn which fascinated my sisters and me as children: 'Within the churchyard, side by side, are many long low graves.' A few Jacob sheep are penned there, doing service as grass keepers. Joseph Paxton's memorial is far grander than those of the Dukes of Devonshire and makes a good shelter for the lambs, all in the shadow of Sir George Gilbert Scott's enormous 1868 church. The nearness of the churchyard underlines the fact that this life is finite and 'in the twinkling of an eye . . .'

March 2006

ACKNOWLEDGEMENTS

My grateful thanks are to Stella Tennant, Ian Hislop, Ben Heyes and Henry Wyndham for their help. Bridget Flemming has taken endless trouble over the photographs on the jacket (where I am wearing the same denim coat that I wore on the cover of *Counting My Chickens* in 2001). Will Topley's drawings are a great addition and near the heart for me. Charlotte Mosley has done her inimitable job as editor. Helen Marchant: I'm running out of adjectives to describe her role in this and my other books; I can only thank her again for her support and understanding. As for Alan Bennett, words fail . . .

The following pieces were delivered as talks or appeared in the publications below, sometimes in a different form.

The Land Agents' Dinner, talk delivered in January 1983
Foreword to *The Small Garden* by C. E. Lucas Phillips (2006 edition)
The Organ Recital, *Daily Telegraph*, 9 August 2008
The Farmers' Club Dinner, talk delivered on 3 December 1991
Derbyshire, *Illustrated London News*, February 1982
Review of *Flora Domestica: A History of Flower Arranging* by Mary Rose Blacker, *Spectator*, 22 July 2000
Book Signings and Literary Lunches, *Spectator*, 19 September 2007

Review of *The Tulip* by Anna Pavord, *Daily Telegraph*, 21
    December 1998
Review of *John Fowler: Prince of Decorators* by Martin Wood,
    Spectator, 11 December 2007
Tiaras, *Daily Telegraph*, 17 March 2002
Foreword to *The Duchess of Devonshire's Ball* by Sophia Murphy
    (1985)
A London Restaurant on Trial, *Spectator*, 7 February 2004
Edensor Post Office, *Spectator*, 2 April 2008
The Arrival of the Kennedys in London, 1938, *Spectator*, 31 May
    2006
'The Treasure Houses of Britain' Exhibition in Washington, talk
    delivered to the Friends of Chatsworth, March 1986
Marble Mania, *Daily Telegraph*, October 2001
Bruce, Mario, Stella and Me, *Italian Vogue*, July 1995
Romney Marsh and Other Churches, talk delivered to the
    Romney Marsh Historic Churches Trust, 1996
Review of *Sassoon: The Worlds of Philip and Sybil* by Peter Stansky,
    Spectator, 12 April 2003
Animal Portraits, *Country Living Magazine*, February 1992
OFTOF, *Spectator*, 7 February 2004
Conservative?, *Daily Telegraph*, 2 September 1993
Debate at the Cambridge Union, *Spectator*, 7 February 2004
Deportment, *Spectator*, 14 June 1986
Christmas at Chatsworth, *Country Life*, October 2005
Review of *The Fall and Rise of the Stately Home* by Peter Mandler,
    The Times, 17 April 1997
Cold Houses, *Harper's & Queen*, January 1987
Home to Roost, *Daily Telegraph*, 25 March 2006

The unpublished pieces, unless otherwise stated, are new.